Gleeson, The Last Vicar Apostolic of All of Alaska

The First Bishop of Fairbanks

By

Carol Louise Hiller

ISBN: 1-4140-2584-X (e-book)
ISBN: 1-4140-2583-1 (Paperback)

Library of Congress Control Number: 2003098764

This book is printed on acid free paper.

Printed in the United States of America
Bloomington, IN

1stBooks - rev. 01/21/04

ACKNOWLEDGEMENTS

Many people contributed their memories and their time to help me. I am most grateful to them all. In particular, I wish to extend my thanks to Professor Charles J Keim who suggested the project and gave initial encouragement along with his guidance, and to Bishop Robert L. Whelan, S.J., who requested Bishop Gleeson's permission and cooperation and gave his own permission to use the Fairbanks archives. My thanks, too, to Father Francis E. Mueller, S.J., Chancellor of the Fairbanks Diocese; and, Father Clifford A. Carroll who welcomed me to the Oregon Province Jesuit Archives in Spokane, WA. For Father Carroll's warm welcome I am indebted to Father Louis L. Renner, S.J., who introduced me there as well as to numerous other people and places. In addition to introductions Father Renner has given direction, help with research, encouragement, and multiple readings of the manuscript. He has exhibited great patience. Many times he has induced laughter in place of imminent tears. Due to his introductions to Jesuit pilots in Alaska I was able to visit St. Mary's and the Sisters who worked with the children there. In Anchorage I was privileged to speak with the Sister Staff of Holy Cross and

iii

Copper Valley who were residing in Anchorage while I was researching.

I have endeavored to walk with and to talk to people in the many places to which Bishop Gleeson ministered. Unfortunately, my legs are much shorter than his so that distant locations like the western Alaska communities were out of my reach. To my Dominican community of Adrian, Michigan my thanks for permissions, time, and monetary as well as constant spiritual support.

And now, finally, I give heartfelt thanks to Avon Overholzer, my computer guru (truly a fundamental concern), Donovan Lumpkin, and Carlton 'Jay' Leith for their invaluable editorial assistance.

Dedicated to

The Sacred Heart of Jesus

With a heart full of gratitude

TABLE OF CONTENTS

FOREWORD

He was the last Vicar Apostolic of all of Alaska. He was the first Bishop of the Diocese of Fairbanks. Catholic schools were a major concern of his, as was the rebuilding and the replacing of rundown mission structures. During his episcopate the Church in Alaska moved from being primarily a mission territory into being a mature Church consisting of three dioceses. His death, at the venerable age of eighty-eight years, prompted the Cardinal Prefect of the Propagation of the Faith in Rome to write, "We have an especially happy memory of the great missionary accomplishments of this excellent bishop." The 13th Alaska State Legislature described him as "a recognized leader and builder of the Catholic Faith in Alaska." But nothing in life so became him as the leaving of it. In the annals of the North, he merited an honorable place—and his life's story deserved to be written.

On November 30, 1976, Father Clifford A. Carroll, S.J., curator of the Oregon Province Archives of the Society of Jesus—housed in the Crosby Library on the Gonzaga University, Spokane, Washington—ended his letter to Sister Carol Louise Hiller, O.P. "As a research worker you are welcome. As a Sister you are warmly greeted. As a Sister working at Monroe [Catholic High School in Fairbanks, Alaska] on the subject of

Bishop Gleeson the doors fall down when you approach. Looking forward to seeing you."

From the date of that letter, it is evident that the biography of Bishop Francis Doyle Gleeson, S.J., by Sister Carol Louise was long in the making. By the year 1976, she had, for some time already, been doing research on the life of Bishop Gleeson with a view to producing a book-length account of his long and eventful life. I, living in Fairbanks at the time, had occasion to help her with her research in the Diocese of Fairbanks archives and to facilitate her interviews with Bishop Gleeson. As one of his fellow Jesuits, I was able to give her the names of many knowledgeable Jesuits to contact for information about him at the various stages of his life. During the summer of 1978, I was happily able to help her with her research in the Oregon Province Archives. The thoroughness of her extensive, painstaking research, both in Fairbanks and in Spokane, is reflected in this biography of Bishop Gleeson.

I first met Bishop Gleeson in the late summer of 1958. His room in Loyola Hall, the Jesuit residence in Fairbanks, was just across the hall from mine. I could not help noticing that his door was always open, and that at night he slept with his light on. His open-door policy was understandable—for he was always most approachable—but why he slept with his light on I never learned. Twenty-two years later—living then in what was at the time referred to as "the Bishop's Residence"—I again found myself living across the hall from him. The door was open; the light was on, whether he slept in bed or sat in his rocking chair praying the rosary. When he was well into his eighties, the sheath began to show wear, but the blade remained bright, reflecting light.

As stated earlier, the life of Bishop Gleeson deserved to be written—and written and published it finally is. The wait of many has been long, but it has been worth it. Sister Carol Louise—one time journalist, teacher and librarian, but primarily historian—has produced a biography of that "excellent bishop," a true portrait of the man, and eminently readable.

Father Louis L. Renner, S.J.

INTRODUCTION

Francis Doyle Gleeson was born in Carrollton, Missouri, on January 17, 1895. Early on the family moved to Yakima, Washington, where Francis attended the Catholic schools. After attending Gonzaga Prep in Spokane for a year, he entered the Jesuit Novitiate at Los Gatos, California, on July 15, 1912.

He underwent the normal course of Jesuit training and was ordained a priest on July 29, 1926. In 1928 Father Gleeson was assigned to the newly opened Bellarmine High School in Tacoma, Washington where he served as teacher and Rector for more than a decade. In 1939 Father Gleeson became Rector of the Novitiate at Sheridan, Oregon. There, it is said, "He ran a peaceful ship, taught the classics and specialized in Shakespeare." From Sheridan Father Gleeson went on to serve as pastor of St. Stanislaus in Lewiston, Idaho, and as Superior at St. Mary's Mission, Omak, Washington. While at Omak, he was appointed to succeed Bishop Walter Fitzgerald as Vicar Apostolic of Alaska; that is, a Bishop representing the Pope. He was consecrated bishop in St. Aloysius Church, Spokane, Washington on April 5, 1948.

The legacy of Bishop Gleeson—a man known for his one-liners, for his taciturnity, for being a man "short on words and correspondence, but long on action" is considerable. As Vicar Apostolic he was responsible, among many other things, for rebuilding most of the mission buildings in Alaska, aspiring to educate the Native youth of Alaska to attain an equal footing with their white counterparts, and giving the green light to the use of airplanes by missionary pilots and to Father James Poole to proceed with plans to establish a Catholic radio station, KNOM.

Archbishop, Francis T. Hurley characterized him as a great gentleman, with the emphasis on gentle. He certainly internalized aggiornamento after attending the sessions of Vatican II.

Don Lumpkin

PREFACE

The sun, already below the horizon at mid-afternoon on a November day in 1976, cast a faint ruby glow upon the snow as I waited to enter the chancery building and Episcopal Residence in Fairbanks, Alaska. A perfect setting for the eighty-two year old retired bishop, I reflected.

I stood contemplating my motives for being on this doorstep at this time. My writing experience to date was in journalism. What worm within swallowed the hook baited by Charles J. Keim, a University of Alaska professor of Journalism, enticing me to write a biography of this quiet, almost mysterious, Reverend Francis Doyle Gleeson, D.D., Jesuit Bishop? There was no time to answer the question.

The bishop greeted me in the reception area of the chancery building and led me to a small conference room adjacent to the large, bright, double-windowed corner office he had recently used. He seated himself behind a small desk as I turned on my tape recorder and reminded myself to speak distinctly to compensate for his slight hearing problem.

To my half-query, *I hope you don't mind being interviewed,* he answered, *Well, I'm not especially thrilled, but I'll make the best of it, I guess.* His answer was no surprise. I knew that he tolerated the intrusion because his successor, Bishop Robert L. Whelan, S.J., suggested it for the sake of an historical record.

Turning his ring round and round on his finger, Bishop Gleeson searched his memory for a considerable time. I soon learned that this merry-go-round with the ring was to Bishop Gleeson as doodling is to many other thoughtful people. Almost tentatively, talking as much to himself as to me, he spoke of his early life as a hazy memory at best and possibly just a hazy memory of family stories told by friends and relatives. And so began a series of interviews that eventually elicited a rich array of information about the bishop's life, Jesuit esprit de corps, and the Church in Alaska.

I was a comparative newcomer having participated in the Fairbanks faith community for approximately five years; consequently, there are areas I might have pressed for information, but did not. Some readers may have questions that did not come up between us, and other questions for which I supply no answers. Nevertheless, to the best of my ability this manuscript traces the life of Francis Doyle Gleeson who administered the Church in Alaska from 1948 through 1968. Characteristically he gave few specific directions, but indicated his desires in a calm, kind manner.

HISTORICAL BACKGROUND

Vitus Bering and Aleskei Chirikov reached Alaska from Russia in 1741. From their reports of the rich fur resources of this land, the crown commissioned fur hunting and trading expeditions. Their Russian Orthodox chaplains introduced the Natives to Christianity.

These were years of exploration by many nations as well as whaling seafarers from the East Coast of America. In May 1779 ships under the command of Ignasio di Arteagas reached Prince of Wales Island in the Alexander Archipelago where the chaplain, Franciscan Father Juan Riobo offered Mass at lower Bucareli Bay on May 13, Ascension Day. This was the first recorded Roman Catholic Mass offered in what is today the state of Alaska. If the Don's flotilla had continued northward, they would have passed through approximately 400 miles of waters dotted with nearly a thousand islands, islands covered with dense, deep green forests of spruce, hemlock and cedar, a result of the mild, moist coastal climate. On the mainland they would have seen mountains rising steeply from the sea, and glaciers moving slowly down the valleys to the sea from snow-capped peaks. Tlingit and Haida Indians, who occupied Southeastern Alaska long before the coming of Vitus Bering, would have observed them from land. It is believed that none of the Natives accepted the coming of the white men.

Sitka, in southeastern Alaska, became the Russian center of the fur harvesting industry. Russian business exploited the southeast and all around the Gulf of Alaska as their exclusive hunting grounds until the harvest of fur bearing animals was no longer profitable. The Gulf of Alaska, on which lies Anchorage, extends from the Dixon Entrance to Cook Inlet as a great curve covering a distance of some 1,150 miles. The curve then curls outward another 1,550 miles along the Alaska Peninsula and Aleutian Island chain. In 1794 the Russian government sent ten Orthodox monks to Kodiak, thus putting their religious stamp on the territory. By 1800 they had made their claim to Alaska strong enough to discourage incursion by other countries whose whalers and exploratory ships attempted landings.

An Oblate of Mary Immaculate, Father Jean Seguin, from Canada made an unsuccessful attempt in 1862 to convert the Indians along the Yukon River near Fort Yukon. Again in 1870 Father Emile Petitot, O.M.I., reached Fort Yukon and returned to Canada with the good news that Alaska was under the American flag. (The Russian fur trade was commercially unproductive, and the territory was sold to the United States in 1867.) Again, in 1872, the Oblates under Bishop Isidore Clut, attempted missionary work at Fort Yukon without success. The following spring Oblate priests floated down to St. Michael on the Yukon delta expecting supplies from San Francisco. The supplies did not come and Father Auguste Lecorre, a diocesan priest, spent the winter at St. Michael while the Bishop returned to Canada in 1874. At home the Bishop heard that Alaska, since 1867, was officially under the jurisdiction of the Bishop of Victoria, Vancouver Island.

Bishop Charles Seghers of Victoria, Vancouver Island, unaware of the efforts made by the Canadian Oblates, began a tour of his diocese with visits to Sitka, Kodiak and Unalaska in 1873. Moving up the Yukon River in 1877 as far as Tanana, he and Fr. Joseph Mandart a diocesan priest from Vancouver Island spent the winter in Nulato. Here they were close to the center of Alaska's heartland which is cradled between the Brooks Range in the north and the Alaska Range in the south, a 166,000-square-mile area drained by the Yukon River and its tributaries. The area varies in temperature from ninety degrees Fahrenheit in summer to minus sixty degrees in winter.

Upon returning to Victoria, Bishop Seghers discovered that he had been named Coadjutor to the Archbishop of Oregon City. In May 1879 Bishop Seghers founded a mission at Wrangell and put Father John Althoff in charge. When Bishop Seghers became Archbishop of Oregon in 1881, he appealed to Pope Leo XIII to be allowed to renounce his See and return to

Alaska. His request was granted. Without the responsibility of the Oregon Archdiocese to circumscribe his activity, Archbishop Seghers visited Sitka in 1885 where he established a mission and left Father William Heynen in charge. Father Louis L.Renner, S.J., writes of the Archbishop: *On July 13, 1886 Seghers set out for Alaska on his fifth journey. He had with him two Jesuits, Paschal Tosi and Aloysius Robaut. Both men had been loaned to him as companions. Their route took them over the Chilkoot Pass, through Canada to the confluence of the Stewart and Yukon Rivers where the two Jesuits, unknowingly on Canadian soil rather than in Alaska, spent the winter in missionary work. In the spring of the year, against the advice of his companions, Archbishop Seghers had chosen to take Francis Fuller, a Catholic layman, as a companion on his travels toward Nulato. Seghers,* continues Father Renner, *was most eager to get to Nulato, for he feared that Protestant missionaries would arrive before him and take over the area.*

As Seghers and Fuller made their way down the Yukon, their boat, traveling conditions, and Fuller's mind deteriorated rapidly. On 4 October they arrived at Nuklukayet where they waited for the river to freeze solid enough for sled travel. On 19 November they again set out for Nulato. On 27 November 1886, with Nulato still a good distance away and travel difficult because of deep snow, Seghers, Fuller and two Indians, who had joined the party at Nuklukayet, decided to camp for the night. Sometime between six and seven o'clock the next morning, the demented Fuller fired a shot into Seghers as he bent over to pick up his mittens. The archbishop died instantly.

The two Jesuits now had no official standing in Alaska. In the spring, Tosi returned to the Pacific Northwest to confer with their superior, Joseph M. Cataldo, to whom Seghers had previously written in hopes of getting Jesuits to work in Alaska on a permanent basis. At Tosi's urging, Cataldo decided that the Jesuits would, for the time being, take charge of some parts of Alaska. A long-term commitment would need Rome's approval. Tosi returned to Alaska during the summer of 1887 with all the power and faculties the Vicar General of Vancouver Island, John Jonckau, could give him. The next year Cataldo named Tosi Vice-superior of all the Jesuits in Alaska with power to settle questions on the spot. Seghers, by the shedding of his blood, laid claim to the title, "The Apostle of Alaska," and opened the doors to systematic missionary work by the Roman Church.

At a private visit with Pope Leo XIII in the summer of 1892, Tosi was told, *Go and make yourself pope in those regions.* Two years later Alaska was separated from the Diocese of Vancouver Island and made a Prefecture Apostolic, the lowest of the three stages of ecclesiastical development of regions.

Tosi was named Prefect Apostolic. At the same time, Alaska was separated from the Rocky Mountain Mission of the Society of Jesus and made an independent mission with Tosi as General Superior. John B. Rene, S.J. succeeded Tosi as Prefect Apostolic from 1897-1904 when Joseph Raphael. Crimont, S.J., was appointed. Crimont reported in 1908 that Catholics in Alaska numbered 13,000: 9,000 whites and 3,500 Natives.

The Prefecture was raised to the next ecclesiastical level on December 22, 1916 when it became a Vicariate Apostolic with Joseph R. Crimont consecrated on July 25, 1917 as the first Vicar Apostolic of Alaska with rank of bishop. At age eighty, Crimont requested a Coadjutor with the right of succession. Walter J. Fitzgerald, S.J. was consecrated in Spokane by Crimont as Coadjutor of the Vicarlate of Alaska on February 24, 1939.

When Crimont died in Juneau in 1945, Fitzgerald followed him as Vicar Apostolic of Alaska until he, in turn, died in Seattle on July 19, 1947. At the time of his death Bishop Fitzgerald had no Coadjutor with right of succession. Consequently, Alaska had no Roman Catholic religious leader from July 1947 until Father Francis D. Gleeson, S.J., D.D., was named in April of 1948. The eleven-month hiatus was a long time. Add the years Alaska's Bishops Crimont and Fitzgerald could give minimal attention to the Vicariate because of the poor health they battled, eleven months was a very long time.

In Spokane, Washington on April 5, 1948 Archbishop Edward D. Howard of Portland, Oregon consecrated Francis Doyle Gleeson as Bishop of Alaska. His Vicariate encompassed the whole of the Territory's 591,004 square miles. His challenge was to rebuild and repair church property, give leadership to his priests and people, and strengthen the faith of the Catholic population. In addition, he strongly believed that the indigenous peoples must be educated so they could live Christianity in all its beauty.

He wanted to enable the Native people of Alaska to understand, protect, and develop their rightful place on the land and the sea, in the religious, cultural, political, and economic civilization of the white man who had invaded their homeland and would not be leaving any time soon. He put all his heart and mind and resources into educating the people of the Church in Alaska.

EARLY YEARS IN THE GLEESON FAMILY: 1895–1912

The Gleeson and Doyle families came from Ireland as a result of the Irish Land Question and the potato famine of the eighteen forties and fifties. This party of Gleesons probably came from County Cork where the family is listed among the "ancient Irish families" as chiefs of the barony of Imokilly.

Father O'Reilly, Bishop Gleeson's Jesuit friend, researched the Gleeson family name while traveling in Ireland and discovered many Gleesons throughout the country. In the Book of Irish Pedigrees by John O'Hart Father O'Reilly found that the motto on the O'Gliasain coat of arms is in the Irish language and translates as The Strong Hand Uppermost.

This group of immigrants first settled in the Springfield or Peoria area of Illinois and, later, moved to fertile farmland near Carrollton, Missouri. Carrollton, the County seat of Carroll County is located on the line of the Wabash, St. Louis and Pacific railroad, 209 miles northwest of St. Louis and 66 miles east of Kansas City. The city, built on a high bluff overlooking the Missouri River bottoms, had a population of nearly 4,000. Here the new comers prospered and raised their children. The Gleesons had wonderfully fertile farming soil on which they raised various crops. The Doyle's neighboring land was a little less fertile more conducive to grazing crops.

When Charles Gleeson took Mary Doyle for his wife, the young couple turned their back on farming. Charles opted for city living and a career in business. From clerking in a store, he learned some basic lessons and later invested in a store of his own.

Their firstborn, a son born in 1891, died in infancy. Two years later Margaret arrived just prior to the economic depression of 1893. Following the two year pattern set by the birth of Margaret, Francis Doyle was born on January 17, 1895 and Anna in 1897. Ten years of excessive heat and lack of rain followed by devastating floods forced many farmers to flee the Missouri bottom lands and contributed to the depression during which retail businesses suffered.

With his growing family and a struggling business, Charles invested in an apple harvest to be sold in Mexico. Their hopes high, Charles and his young family moved to Mexico to oversee the business. His brother-in-law and partner remained in Carrollton to attend to the shipping of the fruit. All seemed to be normal until Mary gave birth to a stillborn son. Shortly thereafter they learned that the fruit harvest that year was phenomenal and their boxcar with a wonderful harvest of fruit was reported shunted to a siding where it stood until the fruit rotted. Disappointed the family moved back to Carrollton.

Charles and Mary immediately enrolled their two oldest children in the local public school where they did well scholastically and showed off the few Spanish words they had learned. Eventually the one-upmanship and thoughts of Mexico were superseded by new adventures. They were something of a sensation the day they announced to their classmates that their father had gone on a train to the Far West. Going to explore!

The children related "the Far West" with exploration, Indian wars, cowboys and other exciting events. In reality, Charles was on his way to Yakima, Washington, another railroad and agricultural region, to investigate a business opportunity. He was gone for a few months, and autumn was fast approaching, when a letter arrived from him full of enthusiasm for the position he had obtained as the Business Manager of the Washington Monument Company.

He touted the beauties of the town and enthused about its rural qualities, noting in particular its population figure of approximately 4500. Charles assured Mary that he had rented a house and all was ready for the family. Whereupon his wife, a quiet and serene person according to her daughter Anna, set about packing the family belongings, arranging transportation, calming her excited children, and closing the house.

Mary needed all her composure when she boarded the train with Margaret, eight years old; Francis, six; Anna, four; and Mary Alice, an infant. At night they slept in berths where the children giggled and acted silly until they fell asleep. Napping by day in prickly horsehair seats set the youngsters to scratching and occasionally to whining. Hot winds, laced with sand, came in the open windows as Mary handed out treats from a hamper she had packed with baked potatoes and chicken, fruit and home baked bread.

That hamper remained a delightful memory to Anna long after Francis doubted his memories. Finally, the conductor called out the North Yakima stop as he swayed his way through the cars. Francis, waving like a drowning man, leaned dangerously out of the window, and Margaret waved just as frantically while keeping firm hold of her brother. Anna looked and looked but could not recognize her father. Before the cars jolted to a full stop, Charles sprang aboard and rushed down the aisle to gather them all into his arms.

Everyone talking at once they trooped off the train onto a low wooden platform. Charles settled his family and their luggage into a wagon then slapped the horse into an easy trot on the wide, hard-packed earth road. He pointed out his shop in the next block and kitty-corner from the station. At the end of the station platform he turned and crossed the railroad tracks then turned again up the first street where he stopped before a white two-story house three blocks from the stone works. They were home! Their home, typical for most towns in the early nineteen hundreds, included a barn for the horse and wagon, a well for water, an outhouse, and a woodshed. To the children it seemed very different from their home in Carrollton; however, the whole environment was different and that may have influenced their perspective.

Within the week Margaret and Francis were enrolled at St. Joseph Academy under the care of the Sisters of Charity of Providence who pioneered Catholic education in Yakima. The children's daily walk to school was on wooden sidewalks above the rutted mud of the street, past a haberdashery, a barbershop that doubled as a pharmacy, a general store, and one or two other businesses. On the streets were strings of horses and mules waiting for leathery looking individuals in comfortable boots and baggy clothes. They came from the nearby mines or claims in the Cascade Range and their animals' packs fascinated the youngsters; whereas, the quiet dignity of Indian braves and their serious families from the reservation just four miles to the south frightened them a little.

Francis entered the second grade quietly, shy, but neither fearful nor visibly excited. Alert and quick to smile, he invited friendship. His hazel eyes took in everything and everyone. His prominent ears missed little of what was said. This was his first experience with Sisters. These women with their voluminous black dresses and covered heads were less formidable to Francis than they might be to a child of today because of the fashion styles. Settling into second grade, Francis' discovered to his delight that his teacher was a wonderful storyteller. One day she told the class this story which he later used in a retreat sermon along with an immediate application in his own life:

A young prince, finding himself in serious trouble cast himself on his knees before a statue of the Blessed Virgin Mary and prayed for her help. He promised that he would erect a beautiful sanctuary in her honor if she would help.

That afternoon, shortly after Francis arrived home from school, the screams of one of his little sisters brought the entire household to the garden. The little girl had accidentally locked herself into a shed. The more his sister screamed and the less success adults had in opening the door, the more overwrought the usually calm Francis became. In his distress he threw himself on his knees before the locked door and promised Our Lady that he would build a chapel in her honor if his sister were safely released. To everyone's relief and great joy, the door was opened almost immediately. To Francis it was a miracle he would not forget; and neither would he forget his promise!

Growing Up

Farmers of Yakima were greatly upset by the dominance of the railroads as they experienced it when they were forced to move several miles north because the rail lines bypassed their town. In 1903 the city feted President Theodore Roosevelt when he visited because of his support of the Reclamation Act. In his address to the residents he praised the Act as insurance for the economic health of the community. He also supported the Progressive Movement as it attacked the abuse of liquor and child labor. These political agitations were not confined to Yakima but caused excitement throughout the country during Francis grade and high school years and eventually resulted in the Eighteenth and Nineteenth Amendment.

Of far greater interest to the young Francis in 1904, was the laying on May 22 of the cornerstone of the new stone church next to his school. He was proud of and impressed by his part in the building as was evident in his apparently casual remark sixty-six years later. He and Francis J. Schoenberg, S.J., a future friend, were walking past the St. Joseph's church when Francis remarked, I helped lay that cornerstone.

14

Over the years the Gleesons moved several times. At one home the owner had chickens that Francis loved to feed. He also loved to talk about them and frequently made them the subject of lengthy sermons. These sermons he delivered to his sisters and their friends when they played "Mass". This was a favorite game during his fifth and sixth grade years Anna recalled, and it always entailed a job for his sisters. They were expected to clear a dressing table on the porch, cover it with a white cloth of some kind, and supply candles and books to make it resemble the altar in church.

The girls noticed that he always wanted that particular table and accused him of wanting to "say Mass" because he wanted to watch himself in the mirror attached to the back of the table. While teasing they enjoyed watching him squirm and become indignant with them. On occasion they would change their taunt to, *You want to play priest so you can preach to us.*

Summers in the noisy, bustling town were hectic for the parents of the growing Gleeson family. Anna reminisced,

We used to go up into the country for a campout. This one year, 1907, I guess we were twenty-five miles or so out of town, an all day trip by horse and wagon. One weekend the kids were tired of camping. We wanted to go home, but our Dad came up and took a couple of the neighbor family home with him and left us up there.

So, the next morning my brother and I were kind of put out about it. We took off. I remember there was a piece of dry toast. That's what we took with us and we started home, walking. I don't know how far we walked, a long, long ways, when one of our neighbors in town saw us, picked us up and took us home. When we got to town, my dad was gone. He was working out of town. My brother and I, I can remember us crawling over the back fence and going in the house. When my dad came home we were there.

My mother, I guess, was desperate. She didn't have any idea where we were and we didn't have telephones to get in contact with anybody. That was one escapade that we were never forgiven.

Although Anna ended the story in a matter of fact way, the reality was rather grim. When their father arrived home, he found Anna in bed with a raging fever. She and many others that year, contracted typhoid from the creek water. Hurriedly, Charles left Anna with her aunt while he rushed to collect the campers. He knew full well that Mary would be frantic with worry for the children who had disappeared, and he also knew that Anna was a very sick child. It was not long after Anna's recovery that Charles health began to deteriorate into a painful battle with cancer.

Adolescence

The boy Gleeson and the town of Yakima matured together. During those years, paved streets, streetcar service, multi-storied brick buildings, and the first automobiles were added to the town. Real estate prices ranged from residential lots for $40.00 to prime business sites for $100.00 according to the Yakima Daily Republic. This all contributed to the expansion of the community and the growth and prosperity of Yakima influenced Francis' life greatly. His father invested everything he could in land and buildings. Population rose. Among the newcomers were Charles' sister and her family, some of Mary's family, and a couple of Charles' former-employees from Carrollton. Amid all the changes what affected Francis most was the building of the church in 1904, and the construction of the boys' school which followed in 1909.

The new school was given the grand name Marquette College. It accepted boys aged six and over and it was the school Francis attended from seventh grade through first year high. An average student, he studied quietly and conscientiously without feeling any need to argue with or question his instructors. Indeed, he looked upon Jesuit Fathers Louis Taelman, Balthasar Feusi and Conrad Brusten as heroes.

They were the men responsible for Marquette College and many of the religious activities in the parish.

During his three years at Marquette, Francis was a member of the Latin class that Father Brusten began for the grade school boys. *Because of that class*, Gleeson later joked, *I never graduated from high school. By the time I got through the grades, I had a couple of years of Latin and then I started a year of high school in Yakima. In fact, I finished about the first year of high school.* He thoroughly enjoyed the challenge of the foreign language.

While Francis worked his way up the academic grades, his father worked his way to the presidency of the granite business and owner of a considerable amount of Yakima real estate. This business acumen made it possible for him, during his final illness, to encourage fourteen-year-old Francis to become a priest if he wished. Even as cancer ravaged Charles health he assured his son that his mother and sisters were financially secure and that he was free to enter the seminary.

When Charles died on June 1, 1909, his tombstone records that he was forty-seven years and seven months old. Francis took responsibility as man of the house very seriously after his father's death. Young though he was his conduct was that of an older man. The fact that the laws of the United States did not yet entitle women to vote or to own land he became very conscious of his mother's dependence.

Anna thought that he took his manly responsibilities much too seriously especially as he monitored the girls' activities rather autocratically at times. Just two years younger than Francis she may have resented his assumption of authority more than the others. At any rate, she recounted an incident that took place just before Francis left for the Jesuit novitiate. She said:

I was in high school. A group of students, girls from St. Joseph Academy and boys from Marquette College, often packed a picnic lunch and took a walk together after Sunday Mass. Because I was staying with cousins for some reason, a Marquette student asked Francis to tell me they would be picnicking on the following Sunday. Francis, I surmise, didn't give me the message after he went home and told our mother that he didn't think I should be going out with "that bunch." In retrospect I guess, that was the last order I ever got from him. I was not sorry. Then Anna went on to say, *Francis never lost his temper because his patience was never tested. He was the boss and we girls always obeyed him.*

Jerry Devine, Francis' nephew, seemed to confirm that statement. Jerry lent a startling glimpse into the bustling Gleeson household when he commented that he remembered his grandmother as always maintaining a peaceful serenity. He described the peace of Mary's house as that of a cathedral. According to him, both Francis and Anna took after their mother in looks and demeanor. *Francis*, he said, *had learned early in life how to confer with authority and then administer it.*

Collegiate Years

In 1911 Francis enrolled at Gonzaga College in Spokane, Washington for the academic year 1911-1912 to finish high school. At Gonzaga however, placement was based on a proficiency in Latin; consequently he was accepted for college level classes. To explain that surprising statement he simply stated, *The educational system was different in those days.*

An all-male grade through college level institute, Gonzaga, welcomed day students and boarders. Among the day students with whom the boarders mixed freely, Francis became good friends with Bing Crosby who lived within a block of the school. Boarders had regular study, prayer, and recreational routines, and they were confined to campus except for chaperoned walks two afternoons a week. On these outings they proceeded in double ranks.

Always there were numerous extra-curricular activities ranging from various forms of ball games to choral and elocution groups. According to the college records Francis, called "Doyle" by the Gonzaga youths, took part in elocution competitions and entered the annual contest in the senior division on March 25, 1912.

He was seventeen and his summer break gave Francis an opportunity to obtain work in a window sash factory taking frames from the machines and stacking them in the warehouse. As man of the house after his father's death, he viewed paid work as a duty due his family. Before going to Gonzaga he had held some summer jobs in sawmill and box factory but nothing he took seriously. Also as a youngster he begged to help in the granite works where he learned enough to finish one stone of salable quality. This latter accomplishment he later put to good use.

By July 1912, with the application for his entry into the Jesuit novitiate completed, the whole family endured a nerve-wracking wait for the results of his medical examination. His mother, in particular, wanted him to be accepted. At the same time, she did not want to think of his leaving home permanently. Finally, word came that Francis was accepted with the proviso that he remain strong under the rigors of religious life. The family was relieved but bewildered by the provision. Eventually, the Society disclosed that the medical report revealed a damaged liver. Francis left by train for Los

Gatos, California and was received into the novitiate of the California Province of the Society of Jesus on July 10, 1912.

JESUIT FORMATION: 1912-1928

California, Oregon, Washington, Montana, Idaho and Alaska made up the California Province of the Society of Jesus in 1912. Men aspiring to become Jesuits from these regions began their community training in Los Gatos, California. There Francis and nineteen other Gonzaga students joined several men from other places and closed ranks. They became a class of Jesuit seminarians who studied, ate, played, prayed and worried together for a half decade. Surprisingly, those twenty boys who entered from Spokane never quite lost their identity as Gonzagans, and Francis soon found that his new classmates were calling him Doyle.

After surviving the silence and intense prayer of a three-day retreat, they were given a black Jesuit cassock to wear. *I recognized,* Bishop Gleeson said, *the cassock meant it was time to roll up the sleeves and go to work.* Rising at dawn (in winter the men were at prayer before dawn) was a true test of vocation. By dressing quickly, Francis could make the Stations of the Cross while climbing up the hill behind their quarters. From the stations an aisle of olive trees on the crown of the hill led to a cliff where the beauty of the valley lay below and the mystery of the morning quiet enveloped him. Then to prayer.

23

A wide variety of activities filled the hours of the day. Activities designed to teach about prayer, about Jesuit history and its life and spirit, and about oneself and one's personal road to union with Jesus Christ. Some lessons took place in a classroom, some in a study situation. For Francis the most joyous lessons were found in the freedom of choir, recreation, and the picking of grapes, olives, apricots, or plums in the seminary orchards. It was in the orchards that Brother George J. Feltes was impressed by Francis willingness to work with diligence rather than with the frivolity shown by those who wanted only to enjoy a day away from the classroom.

Though Francis did not care much for sports, he gave himself wholeheartedly to every game, especially handball. At baseball he contributed competently from the pitcher's mound where, one memorable day his finger was injured by a fast ball. This did not impair his use of the hand nor was it very noticeable; nevertheless, a few eagle-eyed young men remarked about it in later years.

The daily routine gave way on Thursday to long hikes, carefree hours at a nearby lake, or some equally diverting activity. Wise superiors insisted upon participation in recreation as a means of mental relaxation as well as of dissipating loneliness, homesickness, and depression. These recreations often gave rise to strong bonds of brotherly friendship.

The recreations were good for Francis who was tormented by loneliness. His sister Margaret's marriage in 1913 was a poignant time because he could neither be present nor give her away as would have been his prerogative. In 1914 he daydreamed of a family member attending the San Francisco Worlds Fair and surprising him with a visit. No one did. Most especially, he missed his mother, his confidant.

In spite of his homesickness he never faltered in religious deportment as testified by Brother Feltes. Two years junior to Francis in religion he noticed the upper classman and said, *He always gave a good example, always had a ready smile, always was a vigorous and willing worker, always had his biretta on straight.* This last accolade in today's jargon would be saying that he "had his head on straight." The biretta, a square cap with three ridges on top, was formerly worn by clergymen, and frequently by the way it was worn indicated something of the wearer's character.

Francis' studious nature enjoyed the weighty schedule of classwork and study ruling most days. He also relished the periodic individual oral testing. At the end of his second year, he and his classmates were allowed to take simple vows of poverty, chastity and obedience. As newly vowed members of the Community they were called Juniors. Scholastically the Juniors began the study of the classics and humanities. Francis was appointed class beadle. Anna said that this was no surprise because he always, even at a very young age, acted older than his years.

The appointment in no way lessened the fun of the evening recreation when the men spent half the period walking and talking, and the other half conversing in Latin. Along with frustration, the early conversational efforts often erupted in shouts of laughter until, gradually, everyone became comfortable and bilingual.

1917 was an auspicious year for Francis. That year he graduated from Santa Clara University with a Bachelor of Arts Degree and the Juniors moved up to Mount Saint Michael's in Spokane, Washington. Here they wore clerical black suits and were allowed company. By this time homesickness no longer troubled Francis and visits, while heartwarming, were no longer part of dreams.

It was at the Mount that Francis and a group of classmates were walking along the side of the road when an automobile hit them from behind. While Francis was hospitalized with a chipped bone in his shoulder his mother and his sister Anna came for their first visit with him since he entered the Society of Jesus. Anna recalls that it was like visiting a friend. There was no deepening of family ties or getting to know each other better. *Oh,* she said, *he was our brother, but we hardly knew him.*

At "The Mount" the men immersed themselves in philosophical studies. Each student had his own room where, undistracted, he could lose himself in his books, or thoughts, or prayer. For recreation, in addition to the other sports, there was outdoor swimming and tennis. The courts were flooded for ice skating during the winter. As a part of their new status, the Juniors occasionally gave Brother Cook a day off. On some of those days one of the substitute cooks surprised everyone with his French gourmet dishes and Francis himself began to build his reputation as a baker of pastries and sweets.

Upon request, Francis acted as barber for his brother Jesuits. He also left a visible mark of his presence at The Mount in the form of headstones in the cemetery. Generations of Jesuits had been buried at the foot of the hill in the old St. Michael's Mission cemetery. When it was decided to move those bodies, and those of other missionaries who had been buried at scattered places, into ground next to the Mount, Francis suggested to Father Provincial, that a marker be put at each grave and that he, Francis, be allowed to do the engraving. Father Provincial allotted $200.00. With that Francis purchased about forty stones from his father's former partner in Yakima. He finished engraving and polishing about thirty of them while he was at Mount St. Michael's. His simple, clean style was continued through the years and those who stop to pray often notice that all the stones look the same.

Among other extracurricular activities he participated in the choir and its sextet. Just remembering their presentation, in the twenties, of "The Sextet from Lucia" made Francis smile in the seventies. He chuckled when it was suggested that their group was daring, and agreed that they had done pretty well. His own parts were either baritone or bass. Recalling earlier days at Los Gatos, Gleeson said that in 1914 Miguel Pro, S.J., *boasted that he had invented a new word to describe my singing. Roosterful!* Miguel, later martyred in Mexico, was one of the Mexican exiles studying at Los Gatos. Undaunted by the teasing, Francis continued to sing.

When he neared the end of his studies at Mount St. Michael's, Gonzaga University awarded Francis Doyle Gleeson, in 1920, a Master of Arts degree with a proficiency in Spanish.

Mr. Gleeson the Scholastic: 1920-1923

The next step for his class was a three-year break from academic work. It was to be a time for the new graduates to gain a taste of fieldwork in Jesuit undertakings. They went out to new endeavors with a new diploma and a new title. As Scholastics they would be called Mister.

Assigned as an instructor in Latin, Mathematics and Religion, and Director of the Orchestra for the first year high school pupils, Mr. Gleeson joined other Scholastics, Brothers and Priests at Seattle Preparatory School. One of his boys, Norman E. Donohue, later entered the Jesuits and remembered Mr. Gleeson *as one who taught us something in first year without a lot of homework the way you had to do in grade school.* The boys at Seattle Prep also noticed while they were playing baseball with Mr. Gleeson that he had a maimed finger. Smirking Father Donohue said, *I was impressed, but then, I was only twelve years old.* During his second year he recalls Mister Gleeson as director of the school band who had the boys play and replay his favorite selection from the Sousa march "The Monkey Wrapped His Tail around the Flagpole".

Smiling about these memories nearly fifty years later, Father Donohue commented, *Mr. Gleeson was a good singer, and came up to St. Joseph's with the Jesuit Scholastics to sing Tenebrae during Holy Week.* Father Donohue's memories amused Bishop Gleeson, and prompted him to add his own memory of frequently singing duets with another Scholastic at St. Joseph's Church and, while laughing quietly, admitted that he was sometimes invited as a soloist because the pastor *liked the way I bellowed.*

After some thought Donohue went on a slightly different tack and revealed, *When I was in school with the Sisters, one, Sister Rita, had some of us picked out for priests. She must have tipped off Mister Gleeson because he called me back as I was going out for recess one day and told me that he understood that I was interested in becoming a priest. I was fifteen years old by that time and had gotten over all that baby stuff, so I told him I didn't think about it anymore. He said, 'Well, if you ever think about it I would be glad to help you.'*

In those three years at Seattle Prep Mr. Gleeson discovered that he loved teaching and related well to adolescent boys.

Theology in Spain: 1923-1927

As Francis left teaching he prepared to enter a Jesuit school of Theology. Usually the men received placement at a Theologate in the United States; however, there was not enough room in the two United States schools for those men preparing for the priesthood in 1923. It was necessary to send some students to other countries. Consequently, about twenty Jesuit candidates embarked on the converted German ship, Vaterland, a prize from the First World War. They would study at four different schools in Europe. Mister Gleeson and four others were assigned to Oña in the Basque region of northern

Spain. Sailing toward Spain Doyle and his shipmates considered the political circumstances they could be facing.

About that year Mr. Gleeson said, *It was just at the time of a change in government. Primo Guevara had taken over. He was a dictator, something in the fashion of Mussolini. The news of his takeover came while we were still on the way to Spain, and there was some concern that we would not be allowed in, but there was no difficulty. The borders were never closed. It was an enjoyable trip. If anything the uncertainty lent a bit of spice to the otherwise calm crossing under clear skies.*

The influx of American students posed financial difficulties for the Theologates in Europe which were struggling for survival after the devastation of the First World War; nevertheless, the Jesuit schools welcomed the men. The new arrivals in Oña joined the fifteen or so American Jesuits already at St. Francis Xavier College.

Except for the cultural differences scholastic life was much the same as in the United States. Classes were conducted in Latin and everyone was proficient in that, but outside of class most social exchanges were either in Spanish or English. For Mister Gleeson the Spanish was welcomed as a continuation of his undergraduate studies; for others, the difficulty of communication sometimes proved a source of tension, or a reason for recreation to explode into laughter.

Along with the loneliness that plagued him again, dining became a hardship. In fact most of the Americans could not adjust to the Spanish menu of coffee and roll or bowl of mush for breakfast, a snack at noon, and a heavy evening meal at 8:00 followed almost immediately by retiring. Hoping to ease some of his digestive problems, Francis requested that his family send fruitcake, reasoning that it might best survive the long trip. As in most religious communities, the expectation was that gift packages would be shared. However no one expected to be served fruitcake topped with a generous serving of beans. It caused utter consternation among the American men.

As the Americans gradually overcame or learned to live with the differences in the European lifestyle, the years went quickly. Those who had no relatives to visit in Europe spent the summers in various ways. During the first summer, Francis was chosen to attend the meeting of the Catholic Educational Conference in Madrid. Also that summer and the next he spent time in the Turin Province of Italy where he learned Italian through the use of the Berlitz dictionary. Other free time he and Harold Ring hiked through the town of Oña at the foot of their monastery mountain and through the nearby beautiful mountainous Basque region. Then in 1925 there was an opportunity to visit Rome for the Jubilee Year and Francis seized it. He lived in Florence and attended the semi-public audience granted by Pope Pius XI, and a Papal Mass. This was an awesome experience for him; more moving than any of his later Episcopal visits to Rome.

The next year, 1926, course work finished with the students defending various theses. Cornelius E. Byrne, S.J., a classmate, explained a little about the Spanish curriculum. Essentially, it was like the American structure for a Doctorate. Among four courses, the seminarians could study for the "short course" or the so-called "long course." The latter was the challenger and culminated in a defense of a thesis. Gleeson opted for it.

The studies entailed concentrated work, and close preliminary conversations with his professors. If even one instructor was not prepared to defend the thesis, the student might fail. Father Byrne implied that this happened at Gleeson's examination for the "long course." Perhaps it did. From his grade school days, Francis never found it worthwhile to challenge an instructor. At any rate, he failed the "long course." As a consequence, he was denied the fourth vow of obedience to the Pope, a vow that he longed to take. We can only surmise the depth of his pain by considering Francis love for obedience as noted by his contemporaries nicknaming him, "The Obedient Jesuit." Also, Father Byrne emphasized the nickname when he observed, *Doyle never saw anything that he wasn't doing right by doing what he was told.*

Putting aside his disappointment, Francis continued his studies in his usual calm manner until July 29, 1926, when James Gaspar Y Velderish, Archbishop of Burgos ordained him a Priest of God. Neither family nor friends were there to share his joy; nevertheless, his spiritual happiness was great and he addressed himself with enthusiasm to his fourth year of Theology at St. Francis Xavier College.

Tertianship at Port Townsend: 1927-1928

Immediately after Theology, it was customary for the young priest to spend a year at some Jesuit center renewing his spiritual life, dedication, and fervor that St. Ignatius believed might have been diluted by the academic immersion. Father Gleeson applied for an appointment to France for this year in the hope of becoming fluent in French to complement his Spanish and Italian.

Again disappointment! He was told to report to Port Townsend, Washington, where the Oregon Province was opening a new facility for Tertians. Ten men were needed to make Manresa Hall viable. One of the appointees became ill and Francis was designated to take his place.

During his last summer in Spain, Father Gleeson traveled in leisurely fashion the length of the country, preached a retreat in Gibraltar for a group of English Sisters studying there, and finally returned to the United States about mid September to visit his mother and sisters in Yakima. Father Brusten, Francis' teacher and pastor in 1912, was still at St. Joseph's in Yakima and arranged fitting celebrations for his young friend.

Father Francis' sister, Anna, learned of Father Brusten's plans when, *He called me aside and wanted to know if I could meet the train and bring Francis home to stay overnight at our house because the beds in the rectory were full. That was the most wonderful thing that ever happened. We couldn't believe it. In itself, this one kindness made the homecoming a tremendously happy event for the whole family, but there was more.*

Father Brusten, the pastor Anna had looked upon as a stern, imperious German, invited a Monsignor from Seattle to give a sermon at a First Mass celebration in the parish church, and primed the parishioners for this very special event. Following the Mass, Francis' mother and his sisters Anna, and Margaret hosted a dinner at the family home. According to Anna's recollection, their mother did not feel well on the day of the First Mass, so Francis visited with her in her bedroom before the meal. Whatever illness she had, she recovered to live many more years. The home setting, the American food, the family reunion, all etched itself into Francis' memory. During his life he often wished aloud for one bite of chicken as good as the one served at that celebration.

The morning after the surprise party he set out for Port Townsend on the northeastern corner of Washington's Olympic Peninsula. The Port has been described as a waterfront town with the tang of the sea, a million dollar smell from a local pulp mill, and a magnificent view of the Cascade Range, the Olympics, and Mount Rainier.

The Tertian house, a three-story brick mansion built about 1900, overlooked the bay and had accommodations for twenty-one men. Even as the priests took possession, workmen were noisily constructing a new wing in chateau style to harmonize with the older building. Isolated there, four hours from Seattle by ferry or bus, the Tertian Class of 1927 began a year of spiritual renewal and priestly ministry under the direction of Father Walter Fitzgerald who would become Coadjutor Bishop of the Vicariate of Alaska seven years later.

Once again the year sped by. Father Francis made a thirty-day retreat, ministered in a nearby Catholic hospital for another thirty days, and reviewed with intensity the teachings of St. Ignatius and his spiritual way. He did not leave Port Townsend except for six weeks during Lent when he helped in various

Oregon parishes giving about seventy different Lenten talks, missions, and instructions.

Jesuit on Assignment

Bellarmine High School
Tacoma, Washington: 1928-1939

After Tertianship, Bishop Gleeson recalled, *I went to Tacoma and taught in the school. Bellarmine was just starting in 1928 and they'd just finished the building.* He went on to say that the school opened amid a storm of controversy within the Jesuit community. There were three factions:

- one objected to it as an additional financial burden;
- the second feared existing schools might suffer enrollment depletion;
- the third ridiculed the location of the school in the wilderness at the corner of South Twenty-third and the cow path called Union Avenue.

Father David P. McAstocker, S.J., known as Father Dave to distinguish him from his brother John, bought the land in 1927 and built the school as directed by Joseph M. Piet, the Provincial Superior. Father Piet wanted to have a separate high school for boys in Tacoma. On September 4, 1928 six Jesuits and two lay faculty members came from neighboring St. Leo's to meet one hundred forty young men in a neat brick school building surrounded by stone-strewn ground. A boardwalk approached the entrance, strayed around the building, and disappeared into the woods behind. A small construction shack, weather-tightened and shingled for use as a cafeteria, stood to one side tied there by a segment of boardwalk stemming from the main approach.

Young Father Francis Gleeson was one of the six Jesuits from St. Leo's. He was assigned to teach Spanish and Latin to the first year men. Most of his proficiency in both languages came through oral use; consequently, he encouraged the young men to converse as they searched for proper expressions. His classes became known for a constant murmur, and, at times, thunderous repetitive drills.

Seldom did he raise his voice to command attention or obtain obedience. It was enough to give a hard look or a sound of displeasure to bring quick results. Before answering questions, he created an atmosphere of consideration and study by reflecting thoughtfully. The boys sometimes baited him with innocuous questions to which he gave due consideration and solemn-faced inoffensive answers.

Some of his teaching techniques would be frowned upon in today's classroom, as they should be, because he learned them from the Bellarmine football coaches William Hardie and John P. Heinrick who drove the boys relentlessly. Father Gleeson admitted that he had discovered this to be an error when he said,

I got the idea that some of that (football technique) *could be worked into a method of teaching; that is, driving, insulting and beating them down, if necessary. With experience I came to realize, if you go too much into beating down rather than inspiring, you don't get the best results.*

At the end of that academic year, 1928-29, nineteen young men graduated. They had had the opportunity to participate in a complete academic program including a full schedule of extra curricular activities from an active drama and speech department to the establishment of a monthly publication, The Lion.

Interior finishing work continued in the school building, and with the coming of summer, landscaping began and a cement drive replaced the wooden walk to the front door. In the fall, with the Republican Herbert Hoover in the White House, the stock market crashed. All work halted, everywhere. Tacoma, as lumber capitol of the Northwest, was particularly hard hit by the depressed economy. With the resumption of classes in September, many parents could afford only half-tuition payment, irregular payment, or, for many, only a promise of payment. No student was turned away for lack of money.

In spite of hard times, Bellarmine Prep continued to grow. During the school year, a small but adequate faculty residence matching the first building was constructed, and Father Dave, Bellarmine's first Rector, chose Gleeson as his personal consultor. Two years later with tuberculosis sapping the Rector's strength, Father Gleeson received an appointment as Minister of the House. The new title added overseer of all household affairs to his teaching duties.

One evening Father Dave took his House Minister with him to visit a very wealthy family in Tacoma. Father Dave was sure he could obtain a million dollar gift that very night with which to pay off all the debts. The next morning at breakfast everyone was excited about the outcome of the visit. In characteristic Gleeson style the House Minister wryly commented, *During the evening I was not sure whether Father Dave wanted to get a million dollars from Mr. X or to give a million dollars to Mr. X. Certainly, we didn't receive a million dollars!*

His appointment in 1933 as Rector of Bellarmine was equivalent to being named manager. Shortly thereafter, John C. McAstocker, Principal of Bellarmine, was made Pastor of St. Leo's Church, and Father Gleeson temporarily assumed the title of Principal until Cornelius V. Mullen was officially installed later in the year.

In five years Father Gleeson rose from youngest priest on the new faculty to principal of the school. *It was a difficult situation*, Gleeson acknowledged, *because it was right in the heart of the depression. So we had to hang on.* "Hang on" meant to cut staff to the bone, keep a close eye on financial outlays and eliminate waste wherever it appeared. Father Harold O. Small wrote in 1983,

I was a Scholastic at Bellarmine in 1933, when Father Gleeson was eliminating waste in the kitchen. The only kind of cook the school could hire for the faculty house was a man who boasted that he had worked at the Waldorf Astoria in New York, but we were sure not as a cook; perhaps, washing garbage cans. To save money, the Rector made the daily breakfasts and cooked on weekends. The men looked forward particularly to Sunday evening when Father Rector prepared an Italian dinner.

Money was so scarce that Father Gleeson procured some pigs to root through the corn and potatoes growing haphazardly in the front yard of the school, and some cows to pasture on the alfalfa sprouting around the buildings. The Jesuit Scholastics milked the cows and churned the cream to butter for community use. The pigs substituted for "The fatted calf" on special days. After a particularly meager meal, candy bars might be brought from the school store as an evening

42

snack. Benefactors staved off destitution for the Fathers, and Bellarmine mothers of the Philomathea Club ran canned food drives to stretch the Jesuits' per capita budget of a dollar and six cents a day. Mothers also helped with incidental necessities.

The mothers also ran fundraisers to help defray school expenses. *One year*, as Father Philip S. Land recalls, *an Italian dinner sponsored by the Mothers' Club nearly came to grief. The gas on the stove gave out with a hall full of guests. Waiting for the gas to go on, the women of the Mothers' Club plied the company with good old 'dago red.' I came in late and met some guests reeling down the stairs. They greeted me with, "We didn't have anything to eat but it was a great party anyhow." Returning home to Bellarmine with Father Rector, I remarked that we would catch hell when the Bishop heard of this. Gleeson grinned and replied, "Mebbe. But one thing is sure, we won't have to advertise next year."*

As Rector, Gleeson looked for ways to upgrade the school. He encouraged Philip Land's efforts with the students to remove the stones from the playing field, lay turf and install a sprinkling system, and create rock gardens from materials they gathered locally. For his part, Father Gleeson as Chaplain at McNeil Island Prison knew an ex-prisoner he could trust to lay a pool in colored stone in front of the Jesuit residence and build a new altar and altar platform for the house chapel. Some financial aid for both school and students accompanied the introduction of The Reserve Officers' Training Corps in 1935.

The constant need to conserve, to count pennies, to raise money, naturally eroded the spirits and enthusiasm of the faculty. To counter this Father Rector encouraged the priests and Scholastics to mingle during community recreations, a practice not usual in the Society at that time. Between them Father Rector and Mister Joseph A. Lynch, with constant good cheer and delightful repartee, kept the men in high humor. Master of the witty remark, Father Gleeson lost no opportunity to draw a smile. Mister Land occasionally became frustrated enough to say, *When I'm Rector I won't do that*, to which Father Rector invariably responded, *Well, the Society has made mistakes before.* Because he appreciated the men's need for relaxation, he would quietly whisk playing cards, banned in the Province at this time, out of sight when Father Provincial came visiting. The cards reappeared when the visitor departed.

Then, toward the end of his office, he invited several supporters of the school for dinner one evening and informed them of the heavy debt and large interest payments carried by the institute. As a result the people formed a Boosters Club. The activities produced and sponsored by the Boosters saved the school from imminent financial disaster and ensured future solvency. During his ten years at Bellarmine High School Father

44

Gleeson exhibited farsightedness, wisdom, kindness, and poise in carrying out his responsibilities.

Though it was a struggle to make ends meet, Father Land wrote many years later, *We Scholastics could do anything so long as we didn't ask for money. Take a debating team to a regional competition? Sure, if you can raise the money.* The Rector's latitude encouraged some of the faculty to find ways of financing their projects, to become resourceful and cope; however, the easy governance provided little guidance for the less imaginative or aggressive.

Saint Francis Xavier Novitiate
Sheridan, Oregon: 1939-1942

Opened in 1931 Saint Francis Xavier Novitiate stood on a hill a few miles outside the town of Sheridan, a very small town with a gravel main street and, on the north side, many fire decimated lots. The town's water system was barely adequate for its residential and agricultural needs.

A long dusty lane rose abruptly up a hill from the valley floor almost to the Novitiate building before becoming a gentle slope. The Juniorate and attached Novitiate was often called "The Farm" because it was located in the country, in the midst of some eight hundred acres of extensive fruit orchards, timber lands, and alfalfa for the dairy herds.

Standing atop a little hill in the foothills of the Coast Range the Novitiate/Juniorate building overlooked the small but lovely Yamhill Valley, scene of picturesque farms and extensive fruit and nut orchards. It was about twenty-five miles on a direct line from there to the ocean, some forty-five miles by roadway.

When Father Gleeson went to Bellarmine in 1928, the high school was newly built and carrying an original debt which looked manageable in a flourishing economy. The new Novitiate at Sheridan, Oregon was a different story. It opened because Jesuit numbers had increased to such an extent that it was deemed necessary to divide the California Province. The northern part became the Oregon Province and included Oregon, Washington, Montana, Idaho, and the Mission Territory of Alaska.

Those aspiring to serve in the Oregon Province began their religious training and education at St. Francis Xavier Novitiate. Unfortunately, the new province had little money to spend on the Novitiate to fulfill these goals. Providentially, Father Francis Doyle Gleeson, the appointed Rector at Sheridan, came with four priceless assets:

- experience with poverty,

- experience with authority (his own and that due his superiors),
- experience with young men of high ideals and great enthusiasm,
- experience in the use of his ever present wry humor.

He acquired, on arrival, two desperate needs: water supply and funds. According to his own account, the financial situation, though desperate, had the saving grace of being a problem for the Oregon Province rather than for the school. Nevertheless, he admitted, *...the Province was not too prosperous, so we had to get along with very little budget.*

His immediate problem was one of food for the young men. To stretch funds, he visited local cities and towns on price comparison tours. Fishermen at the docks in Astoria, Oregon made his expeditions very worthwhile quoting fresh salmon prices at eight to ten cents a pound, sometimes a dollar a fish. Vegetables were found in the local cities, and the school's location in an orchard area kept the kitchen in fresh fruit.

Recreation in this remote area threatened to be another problem; however, generous donors made possible the building of a villa for the Juniors and Scholastics. Father Leo S. Gaffney scouted diligently for land on which to build a villa and found the perfect piece on the Oregon coast where the Little Nestucca River enters the Pacific Ocean. Father Rector approved the section of land surrounded by privately owned acres and with no access road, and engaged an agent from among the donors to make the purchase. The owners had an asking price of $25,000 at which the agent laughed. He finally obtained the ninety acres for $1,500.

The Judge negotiating an agreement to provide access rights refused the Jesuit application hoping the petitioners would trespass. Instead, Father Gleeson rearranged the summer school schedule. Scholastics hauled supplies in by boat and winched them up the hillside to the building site, and Father Gaffney's crew prepared to build. The Judge knowing himself outmaneuvered, surrendered saying, *Gentlemen, it has been a privilege to cooperate with you.*

It remained only to find a cook for the eager workers. Father Gleeson decided that he would cook thus breaking with a tradition that dictated a different superior preside at a villa to give the students a summer break from the usual authority figure. There were no complaints concerning Father Rector in the role of Villa Superior and chief cook. On the contrary, the builders savored the cooking and cared little about the continued presence of Father Gleeson. The following story told by Father David G. King supplied a good reason for the lack of disapproval.

One could pass the kitchen tent about an hour before dinner and find no food in view and no cook. But, invariably about thirty minutes or so before dinnertime, Father Gleeson would appear and a very appetizing and delicious dinner would be served on time. Cream puffs were a dessert specialty. Father Rector would wait table for the tired workers and would come around to be sure each had enough. He would serve personally anyone asking for seconds.

That kind of service was as much a hallmark of his cooking as the piles of pots and pans left for someone else to clean up in restoring the kitchen to order. Along with cooking, and scouting the waterfront for salmon, he ran errands for materials, kept tabs on building progress and on the doings at Sheridan. Gradually, the double load became too heavy and a Junior's offer to help with the cooking was accepted. The Junior, George T. Boileau, proved to be an able cook.

Being relieved from cooking duties did nothing to prevent the return of school days when construction workers changed clothes to seminary garb and faculty assumed greater formality. This was also a time for new students to arrive. Father Wilfred P. Schoenberg tells the following story about the arrival of seven candidates for the Novitiate.

They boarded a bus in Portland on August 14, 1939 and raised cane most of the way into Sheridan where they made a phone call to the novitiate for a ride. Eventually an ...old clunker car came down. There was an old guy, seemed old to us then, driving. He looked as though he just got out of the back forty acres, hair disheveled and old clothes. He grunted or made monosyllabic replies to smart remarks deriding the car and its condition. He drove us up to the place and he dumped us off without saying a word, never introduced himself. We hadn't the vaguest idea that he was the Father Rector until we went to dinner that night.

On the first day of school, periods consisted of a short overview from the instructor. The classes were called "Schola Brevis" because of their brevity. When Father Gleeson took his place before the Latin class for "Schola Brevis," he said the prayer, sat down and,

I still can remember his words, Father David King wrote, *"cum schola longa sit omnino longa, schola brevis debet esse omnino brevis!" (Since the school year is truly long, schola brevis should be truly short.) With these words he left.*

Behind him hung a vast silence, so stunned were his young men. A few days later in the same class Father Gleeson leaned back in his chair and asked for the translation of "globos flamarumque." The Novices, very nervous, looked at him glassy eyed and blank faced. Finally, he singled out Dominic (Dom) W. Doyle and said, *If you are Irish, you should know this one.*

50

Dom immediately thought of his dad's "great balls of fire" but put it aside as not being possible only to hear his teacher roar, just like his father, *And great balls of fire.*

On another occasion when Dom found himself shaking in the presence of his Father Rector, he might have corroborated the Juniors' claim that Father Gleeson was a *fast and terrible* driver especially on freeways jammed with vehicles. He might have corroborated their claim except that he had the pain of blood poisoning in arm and hand to keep his mind off road hazards. This story is that of a dazed youngster being rushed to the hospital.

When Father Rector stopped the car in Portland, a city so big and noisy after almost two years of rural quiet, he told me, "It's just six blocks to the hospital on such and such a street." I hadn't the foggiest notion of where I was and my heart sank as I closed the door. And then the Rector did a wonderful thing. Gruffly he called out, "Wait! Get back in the car and I'll take you."

It is easy to deduce that Father Rector had a different reputation for each persona he assumed. In the classroom, too, his reputation depended upon the student reporting. The Scholastics nicknamed his elocution class "Toni". It was not generally a favorite mostly because of the teaching technique. As if it were a football play, Father had the reciting student repeat a passage over and over until he rendered it somewhere near an acceptable version. Sometimes a fifteen-minute passage prolonged itself to a whole class period with one person "on stage." The passages were very often quotes from Shakespeare.

Some of his students noted that he would not call on anyone he deemed unprepared, and they liked him for it; others claimed they learned nothing, neither speech nor Shakespeare, nor patience—nothing. Most of the men, nonetheless, learned many Shakespeare passages and acquired a taste for his works.

During one school year Mr. Leo B. Kaufmann had an experience with his Father Rector that left him with thoughts similar to those of the "Toni" students. Assigned to live and work with the Lay Brothers for one month Leo's duties kept him busy during the Brothers' recreation periods; thus, he was condemned by circumstance to a month of silence. One afternoon Leo saw Father Rector leaving for a walk in the same general direction he was going. Thinking to himself that the Rector could talk to anybody, Leo moved into step with Father Gleeson and greeted him. The response, civil enough, warned Leo that the Rector would not use his position to "break grades" to talk with him.

By the time Father Leo told this story, many years after the fact, he had come to realize that his Father Rector was naturally a quiet person who would be the last man to put a student "in his place." He also realized that the Rector's coolness came from a desire to keep the Scholastic and himself out of trouble with the Novice Master.

An instructor of Juniors during the school year and director of villa building during the summer, Father Gaffney's third occupation was searcher for a water supply for the school. By 1941 he had found a supply on Bell Mountain about nine miles away. The water was sweet and plentiful and the money needed to complete a transport project was at hand. When the project was presented to Father Provincial and his consultors, they voted to abandon the project. Possibly the vote was influenced by the unsettled conditions during the Second World War. No matter the reason, Father Gaffney and his Rector could hardly believe what they heard. There was no triumphant solution to celebrate at Sheridan.

In spite of his disappointment over the water veto, Father Gaffney continued to give his all in the direction of the villa project during the summer months. Work continued unabated each summer for three years. In 1942 the interior work called for the installation of refrigeration and Father Gleeson needed to give his approval. He and Father Gaffney thought it would be advantageous to have a walk-in refrigerator as well as a freezer room. Once again the Rector contacted the gentleman who acted as agent for the land purchase. This time he asked him to obtain bids on refrigeration. Over and over again the gentleman failed to obtain a reasonable price on the purchases. Finally, the agent appealed to Father Gleeson for help. According to witnesses the transaction was a treat to watch, a lesson in the skillful use of taciturnity as a business asset.

The refrigeration salesman, a loquacious man, came to present his price schedules to Gleeson. Father looked the material over and held his peace. Nonplussed by Gleeson's silence, the salesman lowered his price a hundred and Father tilted his head and thought about it without speaking. In the end, the man was so bewildered that he lowered his bid nearly a thousand dollars and Father accepted.

Among the many stories associated with this project the following by Joseph E. Perri is rather special.

A Scholastic plumber requested the purchase of ten pounds of lead as sealing material for pipe joints on toilet fixtures. When Father Gleeson got to the hardware store, he proceeded to order the lead. The merchant observed in all seriousness that a qualified plumber would require at least ten pounds. Immediately, without a change of expression, Gleeson replied, "We have an unusually good plumber. Make it twenty pounds."

Work was in full swing on the villa one day when Francis W. McGuigan was party to an incident that he remembered for the rest of his life. He tells this story:

One day in the middle of July 1942 he (Father Gleeson) *drove into the entrance-way of the summer camp and I walked over to him and said, "Father Rector, how do you want these sinks that we're putting in underneath the dormitories cut? How long do you want them, etc." and he turned to Father John S. Forster who was next to me, and said, "Why don't you ask your new Rector?"*

McGuigan says that tears welled up in Father Rector's eyes as he looked like a very deeply hurt and very much offended person. Although it was no secret that one of the seminarians imprudently overworked himself and had a mental breakdown, Francis McGuigan was devastated by the fact that Father Rector was held responsible and was asked to leave. McGuigan wrote about the incident forty years after the event while he was stationed in Alaska with Bishop Gleeson whom he continued to regard as *a strong teacher and a very, very dedicated superior.*

Saint Stanislaus Parish
Lewiston, Idaho: 1942-1946

Whether or not Father Gleeson left Sheridan under a cloud was not verified. He said nothing about his move from Sheridan; rather, he spoke of Lewiston as an up-to-date city, center of a prosperous farming community. His parish, St. Stanislaus, with its Italian mission, Our Lady of Lourdes, serviced the Catholics of the city. He described his parish and its mission as fair sized with the ordinary mix of American citizens. The so-called Italian mission church was originally founded by an Italian priest and so received its name.

Francis enjoyed his days as pastor although he did not consider himself particularly well suited to the position. On the contrary, he said, *I always felt that if I was good for anything it was teaching, and I would be more at home teaching than I would be as a pastor. It's a different kind of work altogether.*

Two assistant priests shared the daily work with him. They routinely visited homes on schedule, and he knew his people well enough to tell a fellow Jesuit that he found his mother to be a saintly woman who took care of her home even though she could not always engage in parish affairs. He also taught religion in the school on a fairly regular basis and attended Knights of Columbus and other society meetings whenever he could. When he was not at a class or meeting he was always missed.

His assistants received their share of his thoughtful attention. A shining example of this attention was the transfer of Francis J. Schoenberg. Father Gleeson drove Father Schoenberg to the train station in Spokane, treated him to a big dinner, and went out of his way to be extraordinarily nice to him. Schoenberg was puzzled by his pastor's kind thoughtfulness on this occasion. He wondered if Father Gleeson thought that the bishop made the change because he, Father Schoenberg, had been indiscreet in speaking about a sensitive busing issue? For himself Father S. accepted the transfer as a part of Bishop Edward J. Kelly's three-year service policy. In reality, Father Gleeson enjoyed the men who lived with him and the people of the parish, and during the recovering national economy with few money problems and a knowledgeable group of lay advisors he could afford thoughtful gestures.

For parish social events he made cream puffs that soon became a sought after item. People were known to attend events as much for the treat as for the socializing. He could be present at the parish bazaars for the enjoyment of meeting his people and watching as his pastry was purchased for its merits. His attendance and attention drew the people to him.

His quiet enjoyment was overshadowed by a great sorrow during the New Year celebrations of 1944 when his mother died on the second of January. He joined his sisters for the funeral in Yakima where he celebrated a Requiem Mass for her repose at St. Joseph Church where Mary had worshipped for forty-three years. She died two weeks before her eighty-first birthday.

His transfer during his fourth year as pastor was as much a surprise to him as to his parishioners. It was a truly sad occasion for everyone. Some of that sadness must have reached the ears of Bishop Kelly because he went out of his way to clarify that the change did not emanate from the chancery office. The diocesan three-year service policy had nothing to do with Father Gleeson's change.

St. Mary's Mission
Omak, Washington: 1946-1948

During a visit at St. Stanislaus, Father Provincial had casually asked Father Gleeson if there was any reason he should not be appointed to the Indian School at Omak, Washington. Father promptly answered, *As far as I know there isn't any reason for being appointed there or anywhere else. That is my understanding of obedience. I'll go where I am sent.*

A short time later Father Gleeson was told there was a need for his presence in Omak, and he went without hesitation. At Omak he found himself once again in charge of a school. This time it was the administration of a co-educational boarding school for Indian children, and all the farming grounds attached to it.

Founded in 1886 on the banks of Omak Creek by Etienne DeRouge, S.J., the mission stood on land given Father DeRouge by Chief Smitkin. Over the years, it had gradually grown into a cultural and social center for the Okanogan Valley and served the Colville and Okanogan Indians.

The basic structure of the mission took form during Father Celestine Caldi's administration. A fire had destroyed the school and museum buildings DeRouge established, and Father Caldi's reconstruction efforts included brick and stucco school and dormitory buildings. The staff consisted of Father DeRouge's Helpers of Lady Missionaries of St. Mary's Mission, and Sisters of St. Dominic from Kettle Falls, Washington recruited by Father Caldi.

Because of several fires the school was in desperate financial trouble. For many of the approximately 150 Indian children there in 1946, it was their only home and their only hope. Not long after his arrival, Father Gleeson protested to Sister Cook the poor quality and quantity of the food. The cook met his protest with a quiet, *When you give me something better, you will get something better.* Once again, Father trudged through grocery and meat markets. After each foray he returned with a truckload of meat and produce. There seems to be no record of his methods for obtaining food and necessities within a tight budget; yet, he invariably came home laden.

Now, having made Sister Cook happy, he proceeded in his financial reconstruction to make everyone unhappy. A hot water supply installed the previous year was discontinued in spite of the impossibility of keeping clothes and bodies clean without heated water. He also prodded the school's negligent farmer to mend his ways. The man had allowed the once productive farm and its buildings to fall into a wretched state of disrepair. In a short time the lazy man offered his resignation.

I accepted it, smiled Gleeson, *though I didn't have anybody else in mind to put in his place. I decided to make a novena to St. Jude, patron of hopeless cases. In the middle of the novena I picked up a Spokane paper and found an ad put in there by a man in Montana* (G. White) *who said that he was a Catholic and wanted a job in a Catholic situation. I took that as a kind of answer to prayers.*

After Father Gleeson interviewed and hired Mr. White, the farm began to take shape again. In just a year and a half land was surveyed and fenced, and an irrigation system was installed with the aid of the boys. Wheat fields came into being, and pastures flourished for the milk cows. Repaired barns housed newly purchased farm stock, equipment, and some cars.

Finally, a small swimming hole for the children was provided. With all the improvements the Indians of the region were somewhat concerned about their traditional place to set up tents on the school land when they came for school sponsored or tribal events. They discovered that there was no need to worry because Father would certainly continue to allow them to live on the land when the occasion presented itself.

Another bit of joy came for everyone when the school acquired a sound projector and a supply of audio movies. Thrilled with the new equipment one of the Sisters decided to clean out the room containing the old machine and discard the whole inventory of silent film. She had older boys start a strong fire in an abandoned well. They fed the flames with film as she cleared the closet. The children had a marvelous afternoon of fun. Late in the day Father returned to the school sparkling with excitement. He had a buyer for all those old tapes.

Along with improving the living conditions, Father Gleeson had time for old friends and always for the children and their parents. Al Best, father of Albert, one of the school children, said that Bing Crosby was a guest at St. Mary's for a month. Francis Gleeson knew the Crosby boys from their days together at Gonzaga in the early nineteen hundreds. Unrecognized by the St. Mary's children or their parents, Bing had a refreshing vacation away from his highly public Hollywood life.

When visited in 1981, the people of St. Mary's remembered Father Gleeson well, and cited stories that highlighted his humor, his kindness, and his quiet spirituality. For example, Mrs. Best volunteered this story about her son:

Albert, ran away from school with two Scriver cousins. By camping out one night and hiking about thirty miles into the hills, the boys arrived in time for a hearty meal with the family who were gathering firewood for their customers. Immediately after eating, the boys' day of glory turned to dust. They were trucked back to school. It was the day before Thanksgiving and Father Gleeson greeted them very seriously. After careful consideration, he told them that they would have to stay on campus for the holiday. Gloom prevailed, but everyone accepted the punishment; however, to the great joy of the parents, Albert was driven home just in time for Thanksgiving dinner with the family. That kindness and many more like it endeared Father Gleeson to the people and children of Omak.

Bishop Gleeson tells this tale about an incident that began with the opening of a letter *On the second of February 1948 I came in and got the mail and there was a letter from a youngster in Carrollton, Missouri, which was my town of birth. He congratulated me on being appointed as Bishop of Alaska. That was the first news that I had had of the whole affair.*

Just mentioning the letter from Carrollton, brought a broad smile to Father's face. The little boy who wrote the letter was unknown to him and surely had someone else in mind; nevertheless, it was heart warming to get a letter from Carrollton. He looked down at his work clothes, and the contrast between his present status as a simple farming priest and the ecclesiastical dignity of a Bishop spoken about by the boy appealed to his sense of the absurd.

Suddenly, he frowned. He recalled his Jesuit Provincial, Leopold J. Robinson, telling him several months before in an unusual confidence that he was one of the candidates recommended for the office of Vicar Apostolic of Alaska. Could it be true? Quickly, he glanced through the rest of the mail. Nothing.

He washed up and changed in preparation for the evening meal. While walking from his house to the dining room, his eyes scanned the snow-covered quadrangle, the buildings hidden away in the foothills of central Washington's Okanogan Range, and so very difficult to maintain in the utter poverty of this Indian mission school. The rutted road climbing to its gates spoke of neediness; yet, the clean and radiant children of St. Mary's School seemed happy and content with their simple diet, well-worn jeans and skimpy shirts. His thoughts returned to the unexpected letter.

He recalled his unhesitating declaration to his Father Provincial in 1943, *My idea of obedience is to do as I am told.* Now that this immense burden of being Vicar of Alaska might be laid on him "by order of holy obedience," he saw his earlier declaration suddenly take on a new meaning. Awash in memory, Francis envisioned his childhood life in a large house in Carrollton. He recalled the gleeful wrath with which he and his older sister, Margaret, and his younger sister, Anna, greeted his uncle's stealing pies from the kitchen windowsill. Just the memory renewed the shiver with which they always anticipated the scolding their mother gave her brother. Oh, yes, they had relished the prospect of their uncle's shame almost as much as they enjoyed visiting their Doyle grandparents' farm on the outskirts of Carrollton.

His thoughts divided between Carrollton and his poverty ridden Indian children as they filed into the dining hall. Francis realized again the courage his father exhibited as a young man. The life of a farmer usually ensured three meals a day, but city life during the depressed economy of the early 1890s was not quite so secure. Francis' preoccupation vanished abruptly as the last of the children entered the building.

He ate his dinner alternately thinking of his first sighting of solemn faced Indian braves standing on the walks of Yakima, Washington or riding their horses in easy dignity through its streets compared to the friendly, warm, worried families of his children at St. Mary's Mission school in Omak. Always, he found himself glancing at the boy's letter from Carrollton and uneasily wondering what it meant. About those days Father Gleeson said:

Maybe that day or the next, I got a call from the Denver Register asking for a picture and information. Still no word had come to me about the appointment. The Progress called and the phone continued with questions. When all this hubbub started, I called the Provincial's office and asked what was going on. They told me then about the appointment.

A little side incident, told by Father John W. (Dutch) Laux, happened in Alaska before Gleeson's appointment became general knowledge:

Father Provincial, Leo J. Robinson, came into the Rec Room...and said, "I wish I had someone to send to Fairbanks and get the dope on what is going on up there."...I (Dutch) said, "I will go." Father Robinson looked at me in surprise and said, "Really Dutch? Are you serious?" I said, "I will ask the doctor and see what he says about it." Doctor OKed it the next day saying that there was a doctor in Fairbanks, who used to be with the clinic in Portland, and I would be in good hands. I went. Before going both Father Provincial and Father Geary told me who was to be the new Bishop of Alaska, Father Gleeson, S.J., the obedient man of the Province. I was to tell no one, but I sure did enjoy myself as I listened to all the Alaskan Missionaries who all had their hats in the ring.

One night there were gathered about fifteen Missionaries at Fairbanks for a get together, Menager, and the whole gang. The only topic discussed was the "New Bishop." I sat back and listened and listened. Only Alaskan Missionaries were mentioned. We went to three or four in the morning. I had my two bits and asked, being a new comer, "Well, are you sure it is going to be an Alaskan? Can't it possibly be anyone else?" I mentioned a half dozen, like Harold Small, Leo Robinson, etc., etc. and then I mentioned Father Gleeson. 'Nuf said. The uproar was terrible.

Ordination Preparations

Confirmation of the appointment caused a flurry of activity. Responsibilities at the Omak mission needed a smooth transfer and that took a little time. Father had been at Omak for eighteen months. In the meantime, the paraphernalia necessary for the office of Bishop and the secretarial duties for organizing the public ordination ceremonies had to be planned.

Even as Father Gleeson began mentally tallying these necessities, one of the faculty members at the Mount, Father Augustine J. Ferretti, S.J., received an appointment to do the behind-the-scenes planning. He later came into some teasing by Bishop Gleeson, who declared Father Ferretti had earned a degree by organizing all the preparations, and dubbed him Master of Lists. The lists referred to included:

- invitations sent to hundreds of people;
- ceremonial, pastoral and traveling requirements. James U. Conwell, S.J., Chancellor of the Alaskan Vicariate, was designated to find these items among the late Bishop Fitzgerald's effects;
- acknowledgements for gifts received from friends;
- teams of Jesuit philosophy students to plan the decorations, the liturgy, and the choir for the ordination ceremony;
- teams to manage the seating arrangements and the printing of programs.

Although Father Ferretti attended to the extensive public relations details and articles sent daily to the Spokane papers, he used information gathered for him by John P. Leary, S.J. There were also frequent articles sent to the California, Washington, Oregon, Utah and Alaska press. Between Fathers

Leary and Ferretti the ceremonies received the most publicity of any ordination to that date.

Father Wilfred P. Schoenberg, Jesuit historian, observed that *in spite of all this fanfare, when Gleeson was ordained, the Community spent almost no money on it. This was typical of Father Gleeson who was known among the Jesuits as a humble, unobtrusive priest, with a deep commitment to religious poverty. Even his official picture, taken on Gonzaga campus by Leo J. Yeats, S.J., bears the imprint of poverty in the war surplus material used as background.* Bishop-elect Gleeson did lose the poverty battle, however, when his brother Jesuits insisted that he wear dress shoes to replace his shoe pacs.

VICAR APOSTOLIC FOR THE TERRITORY OF ALASKA

There was, however, no poverty of presence for the ceremonies on the morning of April 5, 1948. *It was a fitful morning* The Spokesman Review reported in their coverage of the ceremonies. *...the chill sun shone upon the two hundred ecclesiastical dignitaries as they took their places at the main entrance of Gonzaga University and marched down the block to St. Aloysius Church.* More than fifteen hundred people packed the church and stood in most unlikely places to gain a glimpse of the ancient, colorful rituals.

Sisters of the Holy Names and Sisters of Providence, former students and their parents from Seattle and Tacoma, parishioners from Lewiston, children and adults from Omak, fellow Jesuits, clergy, and officials from the Oregon Province and its near neighbors occupied most of the places. Reserved front pews seated a small contingent of relatives who claimed the first blessings and a brilliant smile from the newly ordained bishop. The Spokane Daily Chronicle listed the family as: *his three sisters, Mrs. Arthur J. Hanses and her husband of Yakima; Mrs. W. E. McLaughlin and her husband from, Manteca, Calif.; and Mrs. Laverna Wilcox, of Sacramento* (Margaret, Anna, and Laverna). Margaret's son, Father John C.

Hanses, S.J., pride and joy of his uncle, was also there as subdeacon for the ceremonies.

During the ritual *the sun cast a soft glow through the stained glass windows onto the high marble altar and the masses of white lilies, carnations, pink snapdragons and greens.* Everything used for the ceremonies from the invitations to the ceremonial booklets had the bishop's coat-of-arms designed by Neill R. Meany, a Jesuit seminarian and artist.

A shower of hail assaulted the procession as it exited the church to a throng of well wishers and friends. After photographs were taken, blessings bestowed and greetings exchanged, the newly ordained bishop stopped to visit with a group of children and their parents from Omak, and promised to stopover in Omak to see all the people before he left for Alaska. They parted as people began drifting toward the halls designated for the celebratory luncheon.

The large Lewiston contingent regrouped at a nearby hall, the clergy and close friends at Olympic Hotel in downtown Spokane. There, too, the bishop's coat-of-arms was prominent even decorating the menu. Among the group at the hotel was Father James Conwell who said that after the ceremonies and the big banquet in the Olympic Hotel, *I saw Bishop Gleeson that evening at St. Joseph's and discussed a few matters with* *him. It was the last time (*before he came to Juneau*) I saw him because he left that evening for Omak.*

Harold O. Small, the new Provincial of the Oregon Province, accompanied the bishop to Omak and various other stops. The two had been together at Bellarmine High School, and they had been fellow students and traveling companions in Spain. Now they went first to Yakima for a visit with the bishop's family. They then proceeded to Omak where children, Sisters and parishioners demonstrated their affection with parties at the school and at the church in town.

Afterward the two clergymen took a trip around the Oregon Province to visit the schools at which they had studied. Their visiting included friends and places the bishop wanted to see before taking up residence in the northland. At each place they stopped their friends insisted upon a celebration of the Mass and visiting afterward. Ultimately they extended their journey to include a few (Jesuit) houses, especially the Alma Theologate in California. Bishop Gleeson revealed a hidden agenda when he remarked,

Some of the young men I had known were down there. Some were preparing to come to Alaska later on; so, I went there for a little visit. We had a celebration in several different places. At last we (Small and Gleeson) *decided that it was time*

to leave for the installation in Juneau, so we arranged to come up (to Juneau) a few days before.

Sailing on the SS Alaska

He went on to say that Father Ferretti went to Alaska with them after much coaxing. Their insistence stemmed from all the work he had done toward arranging matters for the ceremonies in Spokane. They sympathized but would not accept his plea to be excused on the grounds that he was still suffering trauma from the near fatal automobile accident he had experienced.

Briskly, the bishop and his companions walked up the gangplank of the SS Alaska on a bright day in mid-May. Bishop Francis Doyle Gleeson, 53 years old, wore his new title, Vicar Apostolic of Alaska, without pretension. On deck amid the noisy, colorfully dressed and excited passengers, the black-clad Gleeson party made an easily identifiable island at the rail as whistles, horns and confetti signaled exuberant farewells to friends on dockside. Finally, mooring lines were cast off; the steamer cleared the slip and moved into the waters of Puget Sound off Seattle. The city skyline gradually receded. Alaska lay ahead.

Because the Alaska Lines' ship was conducive to relaxation and easy camaraderie, the irrepressible Seattle Police Drill

Team and other passengers quickly turned to socializing. The police invited the priests to join their group and were politely refused. Pleading fatigue, the three priests settled into deck chairs to enjoy the gentle swells and tang of sea air. Their friendship went back several years so that conversation was easy and silences could be long or short without any discomfort. That night, and the two succeeding nights, they fell asleep to the sounds of the popular song "Goodnight Irene."

On the way north, conversation skipped from memories of Bellarmine and Seattle Prep to the beauties of the Inside Passage and the marine life surfacing around the ship. They also discussed the homily given by Harold E. Ring at the Ordination Mass. Harold Ring, a classmate of the bishop and the Provincial and well known to Father Ferretti, voiced in his homily the new challenge to the Church of Alaska. The challenge rose from the influx of people and the newly perceived importance of the Territory as a first line of national defense. Anyone acquainted with Jesuits would know that each man has opinions of his own and is well able to voice them as he considers the nuances of the matter under discussion. The three had lively discussions.

Six hundred miles into the world of gentle movement, tranquil green, and warm sunlight that distinguishes the Inside Passage a deep-throated bellow from the ship's horn announced their approach to Revillagigedo Island and its excellent port at Ketchikan, Alaska. The island's fishing and wood pulp industries flourish in the high annual rainfall. The town is built on the side of a mountain just as Juneau is. The streets are narrow and very crooked and there are totem poles everywhere. Noteworthy, in particular, is the hospital that is in charge of the Sisters of St. Joseph of Newark. During the cargo stop the island's two Jesuit priests, Anthony J. Baffaro and Edward A. McNamara, and the people of Holy Name Church seized the opportunity to greet the visitors. They found their new bishop to be quiet, given more to listening than to speaking. At Wrangell, Sitka, and other cargo stops along the route, priests and people who met the bishop were impressed by his serene and attentive attitude.

The SS Alaska came into the Gastineau Channel on the evening of May 24. Evidence of gold mining could be seen to the left in the remains of abandoned mines on Douglas Island. As the eye follows the bridge from Douglas across the water, it picks up to the right the huge bulk of Mt. Roberts on the mainland with its mining scars. In the angle formed by Mt. Roberts abutting Mt. Juneau, the land slopes gently to the channel. Water action fashioned a cove in which the ship dropped anchor before Juneau, the center of the political life of the Territory of Alaska. Juneau grew from a gold camp, to a town, to a busy city; however, it still retained its earthen streets and small town atmosphere.

First Visit to Juneau

At this stop the priests left the ship and hurried up the wooden steps on the hill to visit the Cathedral. Instead of the large church people most often associate with the name Cathedral, they found the tiny church of the Nativity of the Blessed Virgin Mary. Seating might accommodate a hundred people or a few more if they were willing to squeeze together. It was built as a mission church and became a beautiful parish church.

The stop was short leaving little time to greet the resident clergy and note the priest house and the Sisters hospital before the ship's horn sounded. The Bishop-elect and Jesuit Provincial Harold Small climbed aboard once again to continue their trip north through the Lynn Canal to visit Skagway. Father Ferretti remained in Juneau to assist in preparations for the installation of the new Vicar Apostolic.

As the ship steamed its way up the Lynn Canal, they marveled at the size and majesty of Mendenhall Glacier, and watched bald eagles wheel gracefully through the skies. Skagway beaches called up images of thousands of gold prospectors throwing up their tents to form an ever-changing small city in 1898. All those prospectors were feverish to claim their place on the deadly Chilkoot Trail. Fifty years later that tent town of 20,000 had stabilized to become the port terminus of the White Pass & Yukon Route Railway. The tents had been replaced by houses and become the town of Skagway with a population of approximately 760.

Monsignor G. Edgar Gallant and Father Harley Andrew Baker were awaiting the arrival of the SS Alaska in order to take their visitors to Pius X Mission Home for Indian orphans and children of destitute Indian parents from Southeastern Alaska. Built on the edge of town in 1931, the mission, destroyed by fire in 1946, had just been rebuilt. The new facility had opened its doors in the spring of 1948. Enlarged to accommodate one hundred twenty children, the rebuilt mission used the original brick walls that had survived the fire. They enclosed new spacious rooms for dining hall, chapel, kitchen, classrooms and living rooms. Permanent army barracks built next to the original wall became dormitories for the children. Bishop Gleeson, the economy-wise administrator, inspected with appreciation the mission dairy farm that supplied the needs of staff and children and was located at some distance from the school.

The two visitors learned a good deal from their hosts about the people and the history of this small corner of Alaska before returning to the ship. Gallant and Baker, two of nine diocesan priests in Alaska, were rightfully proud of St. Pius Mission Home, as well as their parish in town and St. Teresa Church that Gallant had built to serve the needs of the people of Skagway.

Underway once more on the SS Alaska, the friends settled in for a twenty hour ride to the southeast where they disembarked at Sitka on Baranof Island. There they went to St. Gregory of Nazianzen Catholic Church on Crescent Bay. St. Gregory Church, redecorated in 1947 for its twenty-fifth anniversary, boasted a nicely appointed interior and a new wing to serve as a parish house. Here the visitors shared quarters with the Jesuit pastor, Lawrence A. Nevue and his associate Francis Merrill Sulzman, a diocesan priest from Troy, New York. During the course of a conversation, Bishop Gleeson heard that about fifty children at Mt. Edgecumbe School, several more at the tubercular and orthopedic hospitals as well as the city parishioners depended upon Fathers Nevue and Sulzman for spiritual care and comfort.

From St. Gregory Church to the Pacific Ocean one observes quiet streets shaded by tall trees and beautified by lawns and shrubbery. About two blocks east of the church is Sheldon Jackson College for Native Students, and the same distance to the west is St. Michael Russian Cathedral. From the cathedral on its little island between two arms of Lincoln Street, the ocean and the entrance to Sitka Harbor is about two blocks.

During World War II, the U.S. Navy maintained a base on Japonski Island in Sitka Harbor that included a hospital for Service personnel. When the Navy withdrew its people after the war, the Alaska Native Services equipped some of the buildings and named the compound Mt. Edgecumbe School. The school became very well known. It serviced approximately seven hundred Native children from all over Alaska of whom some ten-percent registered as Roman Catholic. The Navy hospital and some other buildings became tubercular and orthopedic hospitals for Indians and Eskimos. To the bishop's gratification, the Church flourished in Sitka through the efforts of the priests and despite the naval withdrawal and the consequent economic hardship.

In the evening, a call came for Father Nevue through the radiotelegraph service of the Alaska Communications System. The call prompted questions about the radiotelegraph and the extent of its use in the Territory. Later, the bishop would hear from the people in the bush their preference for a radio broadcast called Tundra Topix. Tundra Topix was popular because it broadcast daily and the information was open to all listeners so that a person not directly named might discover something of interest or relevance to him.

While the bishop was visiting in Sitka, preparations for his installation moved forward in Juneau. Hospitality and ceremonial arrangements were nearly complete. Bishop John L. Coudert, O.M.I., Vicar Apostolic of Whitehorse, Yukon Territory, arrived on May 25 to enjoy a few days of relaxation. Gleeson, Small, and Nevue arrived from Sitka on May 28. Father Dermot O'Flanagan, pastor of Holy Family in Anchorage, and Patrick J. MacDwyer, ranking chaplain for the U.S. Army in Alaska, flew in from Anchorage in time for practice ceremonies on Saturday evening, May 29.

INSTALLATION OF THE THIRD VICAR APOSTOLIC

The next morning the skies were clear over the Church of the Nativity of the Blessed Virgin Mary. Bishop Coudert presided during the Installation ceremony with the miniscule sanctuary overflowing with an Episcopal throne on each side of the altar, a Cross bearer, acolytes, servers, nine priests and two bishops. Father Joseph F. McElmeel, read the Papal Bull, the document of appointment issued by Pope Pius XII, in Latin and in English. Prayers for the new Vicar Apostolic followed; then the choir sang the antiphon and versicle of the Nativity of the Blessed Virgin Mary, patroness of the Cathedral parish. Bishop Gleeson descended to the foot of the altar from his throne on the Epistle Side and was escorted to the throne on the Gospel Side where he took his seat and was handed the Shepherd's Crook or Crozier by Bishop Coudert. The Installation was then complete. Catholic Alaska, a territory one fifth the size of the continental United States, rejoiced with the bishop for whom they had waited eleven months. Rising, he gave his blessing, accepted the obeisance of his clergy, and said his first Solemn Pontifical High Mass as Vicar Apostolic.

Father Robert L. Whalen, S.J., pastor at the Church of the Nativity of the Blessed Virgin Mary expected that every seat in the church would be occupied for the ceremony investing the third Vicar Apostolic of Alaska. The small number of parishioners present for the service disappointed him. He excused them saying that the people might not have been sufficiently advised concerning the importance of the ritual.

In the evening the new Vicar Apostolic presided at a Solemn Benediction in his Cathedral followed by a public reception in the school hall. Father Conwell wrote these words to his mother about the formal reception that he planned: *The ladies will pour (with their hats on) and the young ladies, dressed in formals, will serve.* According to church records a steady stream of Juneau people, Catholic and non-Catholic, passed Bishop Gleeson and Bishop Coudert for more than two hours. The reception was a resounding success.

On the morning of May 31 guests departed quickly and Father Small, who punned that he went up to the *insulation* of Bishop Gleeson, prepared to return to his headquarters in northwest Oregon. Bishop Coudert delayed his leave-taking to discuss with his Alaskan counterpart the movement of the Catholic Indians from the Yukon Territory into the eastern borders of Alaska near Tok where no priest functioned. He also took the opportunity to invite Bishop Gleeson to travel with him to the anniversary festivities at the hospital in Dawson in the Yukon Territory. During a briefing after the ordination ceremonies in Spokane, Father Conwell had advised Bishop Gleeson about the anniversary. It was to be a celebration for the fifty years the Sisters of Saint Anne had labored at Saint Mary's Hospital founded by Father William Henry Judge at Dawson in 1897. The Sisters staffed the hospital the next year in response to his urgent appeal for help.

After Bishop Coudert left Juneau, Bishop Gleeson settled into his office on the third floor of the spacious parish house. It was a comfortable place for a missionary headquarters although there was no designated cook for the men who called this home. They had no need for a cook because the Sisters at the hospital served their meals in the hospital. From his office the bishop had a fine view of the town, the busy harbor, and the banks of Douglas Island across the channel. Father Conwell wrote in a letter to his mother, *The Bishop will stay around here for about a month. We are gradually getting a lot of things straightened out. He seems to be very easy to work with.*

This was a time for getting acquainted: Bishop Gleeson with his chancellor and the priests of the parish and they with him. In addition the bishop studied reports, listened to his chancellor's briefings, and sent letters to missionaries in the north, answering their questions and asking them when he should plan to visit. The Fathers said Gleeson's letters were always brief and to the point with questions or messages treated thoroughly in spite of the brevity.

It would take some time for the newness to wear off and for the Vicar to saturate himself in the workings of this huge territory of which he had become the Shepherd. By visiting the missions as he journeyed up the Inside Passage, he had made a beginning toward understanding some of the management problems and requirements of his priests and pastors. He had yet to see the greater and poorer area of Alaska. His task would be to know the men working on the missions, their worries, their strengths and weaknesses in solving their personal and mission problems, their need for specific direction or support if that existed.

And all of that depended upon his own strength and understanding and his ability to draw the best from his pastors for them and for their people. Some of the priests warned the bishop that weather and transport made it difficult to set any specific dates or times for travel and arrival. One of the many documents the bishop studied was a list of the missions and their personnel. That, along with a map, determined the schedule for visits during the next months.

Bishop Gleeson Voices His Goals

It is unquestionably a high honor to be made a bishop. It is an honor to be given the fulness of the priesthood, to become a successor of the Apostles, to be a member of the teaching body of the Church, to be empowered to administer the sacraments of confirmation and to ordain men to the priesthood, to be made a Vicar of the Vicar of Christ. It is a special honor, I believe, to be given this office in Alaska for Alaska, I am sure, loomed high in the vision of Christ Our Lord when at the last Supper he told the Apostles, "You shall be witnesses to me in Jerusalem and Judea and to the uttermost parts of the earth!" What part of the earth was so remote from the presence of Christ as he spoke those words?

*Though it is an honor to be Bishop of Alaska, it is at the same time a tremendous responsibility and a burden. **By the office I become responsible in a very special way for the well being of the Church in a vast territory. I must find a means to continue and to expand the work so well and so heroically begun by the missionary sisters and priests and bishops of the past.** Heavy as this burden is I know that in carrying it I shall find happiness. Thousands of men, women and children will come to Alaska...All of them will be in search of happiness...but, alas many of them will never*

84

find happiness that will last for they have never come to realize that such happiness comes not from what one gets for himself but from what he gives to another.

Responsibilities

Wherever possible, the bishop helped with parish duties. On June 13 he said Mass and preached at the church in Douglas. He spoke of his responsibilities to the Church of Alaska, and the impossibility of doing any good in teaching and preaching the Gospel unless a loyal and devoted laity lived an exemplary life. He also cautioned about example when he said,

The thing that affects many people most is the example of Catholic people. How does the Church influence their lives? I have known men who have remained out of the Church for years even after being convinced of the truth of the Church simply because they could not reconcile the teachings of the Church with the practice of some of its members. ...

I count on you members of the Church to do your part by prayer and good example, by knowing your faith and appreciating it and being able to give an account of it when occasion arises.

Two weeks later, he conducted a day of recollection at the Shrine of St. Therese for a group of women from the Douglas and Juneau parishes. At this time it came to his attention that the Sisters of St. Ann, who staffed the hospital adjacent to the parish church, had vacationed for five days at the Shrine without the benefit of a priest. The bishop was most unhappy. *The priests were never too busy for this task,* he maintained; *The Sisters had only to ask.*

Quiet time in Juneau came to an end that July. The previous March, Father Conwell had received an informal invitation to the Golden Jubilee celebration of the founding of St. Mary's Hospital in Dawson. To it he replied, *I am confident that he (our new Bishop) will send a representative of the Jesuit Fathers to your celebration.* This was the celebration Bishop Coudert referred to when he invited Bishop Gleeson to travel with him to Dawson. Bishop Gleeson accepted Coudert's invitation and now appointed himself the representative that Conwell had promised.

A First Airplane Ride

He traveled with Father Joseph McElmeel, S.J., who had been invited to address the celebrants because of his twenty-four year tenure in Alaska. They flew to Whitehorse, Yukon Territory.

This, Gleeson's first flight, must have been memorable if only for the air view of Juneau and its environs. Typically, his only comment, *That was the first time that I had been on a plane. The beginning of a lot of rides.* He did admit that the presence of Father McElmeel gave him a sense of security.

In Whitehorse they joined Bishop Coudert for the riverboat trip down the Yukon River to Dawson arriving in good time for the celebrations on July 11-13. Practically all *the Oblates of Mary Immaculate from the Northwest Territory were there for the occasion. It was quite a celebration,* was Gleeson's accolade. He was unable to understand a good bit of the French conversation, but that did not bother him. He enjoyed listening and observing as much as most people enjoy taking part in conversation, and there was much hilarity for him to delight in.

Hardly home long enough to pack another bag he and Father Henry L. Sweeney went to Ketchikan on the eighteenth for the Silver Anniversary of the founding of Little Flower Hospital. Then, shortly after returning from Ketchikan, the bishop was on his way again. He said, *That summer, after getting back, I made my first visit to the missions of the north. My objectives for this visit were to learn the missionaries' needs for the development of the church both in building its membership and extending its education, and to administer the Sacrament of Confirmation. I flew from Juneau to Anchorage.*

Visitations in the North

The first stop was in Cordova where he found the city built on a mountainside overlooking Prince William Sound and Spike Island with the pale green waters of Eyak Lake sparkling in the north. The town that began as a port city for the copper mines of the interior had slowed to a resort town with the cessation of mining, and was, at the time of the bishop's visit in 1948, home to a Catholic community alive, well, and financially independent.

Continuing his visitation he reached Seward on July 25, and Palmer on the 26th. Both were stops on his way to Providence Hospital in Anchorage. From July 28 to August 1, he visited St. Mary's Kodiak where he saw new church buildings, and a flourishing community of faith. The parish membership consisted primarily of commercial fishing people and affiliates of the large Coast Guard base.

Impressed with these parishes, he was yet wholly unprepared for Anchorage. The city surprised him with its vitality and population of over 11,000. To accommodate the growth, Dermot O'Flanagan, pastor of Holy Family, was in the process of building a larger church when a shortfall in funds brought work near a standstill.

When Bishop Gleeson arrived he declared himself willing to help and approached a bank for a loan only to learn that he had no authority to borrow until he was confirmed as executive of the Catholic Society of Alaska. Frank A. Boyle, Secretary of the Society, called a special meeting of the Board of Trustees, at the request of Father Conwell. They, in turn, considered the bishop's request for proof of his authority and instructed the Secretary to send the bishop a copy of the Papal Bull confirming his appointment as Bishop of the Vicariate of Alaska, and a certified copy of the by-laws of the Catholic Society of Alaska. In the by-laws the Trustees empower the bishop to act as President and exercise all powers conferred by the laws of Alaska.

With his authority established, Bishop Gleeson entered into negotiations with the First National Bank of Anchorage to borrow sufficient funds for the completion of Holy Family Church. Church funds in hand, Father O'Flanagan next mentioned that he had not been to his home in Ireland nor seen his mother in sixteen years. He conceded that part of the problem had been the lack of a priest to substitute while he was away. Quietly the bishop considered this and asked if there was anything else Father would like to ask about. Then the bishop sat for some time studying his hands and looking into the distance before nodding and promising to substitute while Father went to visit his mother in Ireland.

Dillingham

Taking flight for Dillingham on August 3, via Alaska Airlines Gleeson had no idea that this flight would prove to be the outstanding memory of the whole north Alaska visit. He had to wait over at the air base in Naknek to get a plane for the passage across Bristol Bay to Dillingham. In his usual understatement he described the experience, *I had to wait several days there. The accommodations were not very good.* Not very good, indeed! In fact, pilots waiting over between trips shared a bunk in a shelter and there was little else. No village, no residents.

Of the flight to Dillingham he says, *I'll always remember, we landed on the water and the fellow couldn't get in close enough to the bank for us to get off on foot, so he came alongside the plane and took me piggyback to the bank.* To properly enjoy the story one must close one's eyes and imagine the bishop with his feet hiked above water level and his five feet ten and a half inches two hundred thirty-five pounds clinging to the back of his pilot as the man struggled to wade through the waters of Nushagak Bay.

In February 1948 Father Paul C. Deschout, S.J., Superior of the Missions in Alaska, transferred Father George S. Endal, S.J., to Bristol Bay from his mission at Alakanuk with its established school. Shortly thereafter, Father Endal received word to wait until the new bishop was installed. When Bishop Gleeson confirmed the appointment, Father immediately moved to Dillingham on the southern coast of Alaska and opened a mission. The purpose of the new mission was to give spiritual sustenance to the Bristol Bay area men in the fishing industry. The nearest Catholic priests to Dillingham were in Bethel, 200 miles, or in Kodiak, 200 miles, or in Anchorage, 300 miles plus.

To build a parish Father had to meet the people in the street or any gathering place and reach out a helping hand. The Native people of the region were primarily Russian Orthodox who had been without a priest for a long time. During the fishing season many of the fishermen and canners were Eskimo people who came from the whole southwestern region of the peninsula and as far north as the Roman Catholic community of Akulurak. These, too, had no one to serve their spiritual needs.

Father Endal worried about these seasonal workers, not only because they were deprived of religious comfort and direction while away from home, but also because three unions, CIO, AFL, and ILWU were vying for their membership.

He suspected that the ILWU (International Labor Workers Union) was a Communist run organization and the Native people would be unaware of the danger it posed for them. This was a distinct possibility considering the aggressive activity of the Party during the forties.

Bishop Gleeson recognized the implications of this apostolate and Father's determination to *see that the Native workers got all that was coming to them*. For many years the bishop quietly backed Father Endal's efforts in the Bristol Bay area in spite of opposition from Jesuit missionaries and union officials.

In addition to their mission work and union activity Fathers Endal and Jules M. Convert, S.J., of Kashunak, a Hooper Bay mission, attended a missioners' meeting at which the Bristol Bay salmon canneries had a man explain the work opportunities for the Natives and ask for collaboration by the missionaries. The priests were not enthusiastic; however, Convert supported the idea on the premise that the Eskimos were bound to hear of the work offer sooner or later. He reasoned that the missionaries ought to encourage the recruiting of workers and send someone to see at firsthand the working conditions.

Convert said that it was not long after that Bishop Gleeson asked *if I'd be willing to go to Bristol Bay for the season since* the Industry had offered him board, room and transportation for a missionary to accompany the men. And so I became some sort of industrial chaplain and spent the season traveling by the Companies' boats from one cannery to the other (some 17 of them all around the Bay). Convert then reported his findings to the companies and they actually acted on some of his suggestions.

While speaking of his recollections of that time, Bishop Gleeson simply passed off the visit to Dillingham with: *Those were fairly lively days in Dillingham on account of the fisheries, but there was no big hassle. They were getting along fairly well.*

(By evening) I finished my work there and was ready to come back. We came down to the water's edge at Dillingham to get on the pontoon plane, and the pilot that was going to fly me back wasn't the same one that took me over. He had quite a bit of trouble getting off the water. He flew all around in every direction, but he finally made it and just barely skimmed over the top of some trees. After we got into the clear, he turned around and said, 'Well, we made it all right, but this is the first time I've ever taken off on pontoons."

Bethel

Once safely airborne they flew to Bethel about seventy-five to one hundred miles upriver on the Kuskokwim River. Bethel has an off-loading dock for ocean going steamers from Seattle. Father Segundo Llorente, S.J., described Bethel in a few words; *It is a flat, bleak land with the evils of the permafrost. Nothing grows there.*

At the time of the bishop's first visit, Bethel consisted of rutted mud streets, army built Quonset huts and government administration buildings, a general store, a school and a Bureau of Indian Affairs Hospital to service Natives of the whole southwest area of Alaska. In addition there was a Moravian and a Roman Catholic Church. The Catholic Church and its priest residence was a Quonset hut too small for the post-war population.

Although the war brought some Roman Catholic workers to whom a Jesuit priest ministered, the Moravian Church dominated the town. The Roman Catholic priest at this time was Father Segundo Llorente. He traveled the Kuskokwin River regularly to visit villages (Kalskag, Aniak, Akiak, Crooked Creek) along a 500 mile length of the river as far as McGrath in the Kuskokwim Mountain region.

Father Llorente spoke of the bishop's visit. As he remembered, *The Bureau of Indian Affairs (white officials) invited Bishop Gleeson and me to a dinner party on the evening of the bishop's arrival. The officials were greatly impressed by him, and it surprised me that the bishop could talk so little and still manage to make a good impression.* Father speculated that Bishop Gleeson's kindly look and eyes that showed that he was missing nothing created the good impression.

For the five days of his Bethel visit, Bishop Gleeson headquartered at a BIA official's home because the priest's quarters were too small. Before they parted that first night, Gleeson shocked Father by saying, *You will preach at my Mass tomorrow.*

For departure from Bethel Bishop Gleeson scheduled himself to leave in time to reach Mountain Village by August 8. He had neglected to answer the invitation to the Eskimo Convention at Pilot Station sent by Father John P. Fox, S.J., in February 1948, months before the bishop's installation. It did not matter. They had been friends from student days and Father Fox was expecting him.

After waiting all day in Mountain Village to welcome the bishop, Father left in the evening to officiate at services for his people in Pilot Station. The bishop, meanwhile, was en route in a small plane that flew low across gray tundra dotted with an occasional low gray shrub and threaded by twisting streams. It was a continuous gray scene affording nothing to aid a pilot on an equally gray day. The plane arrived at Mountain Village late in the evening on August 8 just after Father Fox had sped away. Displaying typical Alaskan courtesy, a pilot going up the Yukon dropped down at Pilot Station to alert Father of the bishop's arrival.

Immediately, Father jumped into his mission boat, The Ark, skimmed recklessly about twenty-five miles down river and arrived at Mountain Village shortly after midnight. Bishop and priest stayed over for a day during which Father warned his guest that he would find some of the Natives living in mud huts in very primitive conditions. However, he said that the people of Pilot Station lived in houses. Their tour of Mountain Village completed, they boarded The Ark and left for the Eskimo Convention.

An Eskimo Convention

For the Eskimo people from Mountain Village and four adjacent villages along the Yukon, the Convention was meant to be a time of spiritual and social rejuvenation. Each convention had a theme and this year the theme on each of the three days was: 1) We Owe God Adoration, 2) Reparation,

3) <u>Thanksgiving</u>. The daily order for the three days: Morning prayer and Mass at 8:00 a.m. with Holy Communion for all; general meeting and main talk at 2:00, with Benediction preceded by beads at 5:00 p.m.

As the purpose of the convention was partly social, plenty of time was left free for visiting, meals and the like. The final service was topped off by the taking of a picture of the whole crowd, or at least everyone who could squeeze in.

The presence of their bishop added a special dimension to the festivities. Everyone felt that the bishop honored the village by Confirming those ready to receive the sacrament, and he honored by his presence a young couple who were exchanging marriage vows.

As if this were not enough, he asked if the people would consider making welcome a community of Sisters if one were to come. After solemn deliberation, the men agreed to prepare a home and supply firewood for Sisters if they would come, and then the matter was left to God. Nothing came of this preliminary inquiry, but a seed was planted and would grow in time in an unexpected way.

After the Convention, Brother Alfred T. Murphy, S.J., and Father Norman Donohue from Akulurak took the bishop with them on the boat, the Sifton, to visit fish camps on the lower Yukon. The mouth, or delta, of the river, known as the lower

Yukon, spreads out for sixty miles and has dozens of sloughs, and creeks running through the tundra on each side of the main channel. Fish camps, or temporary villages multiply on these waterways, and the river supplies the Eskimos with sustenance year round. As the Sifton visited these camps, Mass was celebrated on the boat at each site until they reached Alakanuk, the largest village. Father Donohue told this Brother Alfred Murphy, S.J., story about the Alakanuk stop:

We came to Alakanuk, which was the largest village, so there we had Mass in the church. I (Donohue) *went up to get the church ready, build a fire and so on, and the bishop stayed on the boat. Bishop stayed down in the kitchen and the Eskimos came down to look at the new bishop. They weren't talking at all. Murphy might say hello to them, and they'd answer because they knew him, but, Murphy thought, the only way they would talk to the bishop or the bishop to them was for Murphy to leave. So, he went up to the pilothouse. More people came on and he still didn't hear any talking; didn't hear a sound; the bishop just sat there and the people looked at him and he looked at them.*

When there was nothing to say, nothing was said. Both the people and their bishop understood the value of silence. That is not to say that the Native peoples could not speak, they just did not speak to people (especially white people) that they did not know.

A New Perspective on Church Law

These visits along the Yukon gave the bishop pause for thought regarding the Sunday Mass obligation. The Native peoples had no concept of obligation for Sunday observance. When the priest came to camp or church, the people also came for Confession, Mass, and instruction. When there was no priest there was no obligation.

A further observation during this initial visitation found its way into a letter to Conwell where Bishop Gleeson wrote, *These missions are pretty primitive, but not as bad as I expected.* He did not elaborate on "pretty primitive"; nevertheless, when a people count a stream as running water, a bucket in the corner as plumbing, and a wood burning pot bellied stove as central heating, it is not difficult to envision their primitive dwelling.

Akulurak

Finally, the Sifton reached St. Mary's Mission in the delta of the Yukon. Summer was a wonderful time to see St. Mary's for what it was. Built in the latter part of the eighteen hundreds to give shelter to children orphaned by the flu epidemic, the structures, like those of many other missions, were built on permafrost ground. Permafrost is likely to appear in very cold regions where the ground might freeze solid in layers of ice and clay for more than 1700 feet below the surface. When man builds heated structures on permafrost a hole with water, clay, mud and stones appears beneath the structure. Later foundations stood on bedrock or several feet above ground, but many old Alaskan buildings were constructed at ground level. These places often resorted to putting jacks beneath the building and adjusting the jacks at the change of season to keep the frame relatively straight. St. Mary's was one such old building on which repeated adjusting represented a great danger because the building warped a bit each year and was now twisting apart. Bishop Gleeson noticed and understood the situation at once.

After a short stay at St. Mary's, the group proceeded up the Yukon to Holy Cross, a river ride of approximately three hundred miles. Above the delta site of Akulurak, the Sifton traveled south some fifty miles before finding an easterly course. The scenery changed from marshy delta land to low hills on the north side, and on the south side, to flat, treeless tundra. The desert-like tundra was scored by spring floods through which rivers and streams flowed quietly alongside and between dry riverbeds left after the rush of spring waters cut new courses across the plain. On the north the land gradually rose into hills with growths of berry bushes and trees. Streams carried run off water down hills to more stable channels that added their waters to the Yukon.

The boat passed Pitkas Point, Pilot Station and Marshall without stopping on the way up river. Then, the river skirted an outcrop of hills before it turned north near the juncture of the Innoko River which spilled out of the Kuskokwim Mountains and into the Yukon. The Sifton finally drove into a long channel leading to the north.

Holy Cross Mission

Almost immediately, on the western grassy shore, Holy Cross Church and school buildings appeared. In 1888, on the site of an old Indian village, two Jesuits raised their tent and before the year was out three Sisters of St. Ann and four Jesuits had small primitive houses. From such as this grew Holy Cross the largest boarding school in the interior, where Eskimos and Indians, traditional enemies, lived and worked together in peace.

Once famous for its gardens and vegetable farm, sixty years of harsh weather and spring run-offs had eroded the topsoil, and the Yukon had cut its way to the east leaving a landing site of silt and mud where there had been a deep water approach.

Aware of its past glory, the bishop toured the compound with a great deal of interest. He marveled at the timeworn buildings and the efforts made to bring the school up-to-date. He recognized the enviable reputation of the Holy Cross community.

Serious and thought provoking as the visit proved, most memorable was an incident during the children's welcome and presentation ceremony for the bishop. Sister George Edmond said that everyone was excited when they heard the bishop was coming to visit. They immediately began planning how they could best welcome him and determined that they would present him with a complete winter outfit of fur hat, parka, beaver mitts, and a pair of mukluks. All of these items were hand made by the girls under the supervision of the Sisters.

The gifts were put on a sleigh that two little girls were selected to pull into the auditorium. Scrubbed to a shine and in their best clothes, the children waited their cue to enter. When it came, they started forward. Suddenly, when they could see the bishop, one of the girls dropped her ribbon and ran away as fast as she could. Her partner called after her, *Don't be afraid. It's only the bishop.* The hall reverberated with laughter. Immediately the bishop stood and scooped the outspoken child into his arms for a big hug.

Later, with a tinge of sadness in his voice, Bishop Gleeson spoke about the reserve children showed toward him and his own restraint with them. He said, *I always did enjoy youngsters although I don't get close. I don't know how much they like me.*

Kotzebue and Nome

As much as he enjoyed visiting at Holy Cross Mission, it was necessary to continue his journey around the Vicariate. From Holy Cross he took a plane beyond the Arctic Circle to St. Francis Xavier Mission in Kotzebue where the sun was waning toward the six week period of sunless days from December through the middle of January. Kotzebue, according to The Alaskan Shepherd is located on a spit of land that is about three miles long, 1100-3600 feet wide and about twenty-six miles north of the Arctic Circle. In Kotzebue Sound facing the Chukchi Sea, the town began in the 1800s as a trading post for Arctic and Siberian Eskimos. It had in 1948 an airfield and a sizable white population. The church, big enough for the Catholics in town, was difficult to heat. Parish membership consisted mostly of white settlers, enough to keep a priest busy whose parish comprised all the land above the sixty-sixth parallel, an area about the size of France, with about 6000 persons scattered into tiny villages.

The bishop next touched down in Nome where an active Catholic population had put up a relatively new church built between 1945 and 1947 by Father Edmund A. Anable, S.J., with the help of his Eskimo people.

A leftover from the gold rush, the town began on the non-productive land protected from seawater by a well-placed seawall. After the gold rush mostly government officials and their suppliers such as grocers, clothiers, teachers, and hospital people were the only remaining inhabitants. In the 1970s the town had changed very little. Most of the streets were unpaved and the town could be walked through and around at a leisurely pace in about a half-hour. Airport facilities brought some added population. King Island and Diomede Island Eskimos pitched their tents or made their homes on the flat reaches of land to the east of town when they used Nome as a gathering place.

Father Thomas P. Cunningham, S.J., who welcomed Bishop Gleeson on this first visit in 1948, later wrote to Father Small:

I had a very pleasant visit with the new Bishop last summer. He fits your description all right. Very anxious to help, but has a mind of his own and wants to know the circumstances before making any judgments. I think he is an ideal man on the job. Certainly easy to entertain.

On the way east from Nome, the bishop stopped at Nulato, an Indian village, and the site of the first Jesuit mission in Alaska. Its boarding school, and church and houses were in fair condition considering their age. The Sisters of St. Ann taught in the school.

Now on the last lap of his journey the bishop was back to the Yukon River approximately two hundred fifty miles north of Holy Cross. Here the river turned to the east and passed Koyukuk on its northwest bank. Traveling east for about two hundred miles, the journey was broken with visits at the small Indian villages of Galena, Ruby, and Tanana. Each village had its welcome, its Confirmation class and its get acquainted visit. The flight now left the river to head southeast another hundred fifty miles or so to Fairbanks.

The Largest City in the Interior

Fairbanks, the hub and largest city in the interior, began as a gold rush town, and had the added advantage of its location on the Chena River. It flourished because the river gave people from every direction easy access for trading. The town expanded, with a military presence during the Second World War. When Bishop Gleeson visited in 1948, the population stood at 5771. It had an active business community, railroad depot, public schools, a military and a civilian airfield, and on its outskirts, a university, and two large military bases. Essentially, it consisted of white residents with a small group of Native inhabitants neither absorbed by the white society nor able to cope with its alien customs and mores.

The Roman Catholic community worshiped at the Church of The Immaculate Conception founded in 1904 by Father Francis M. Monroe, S.J. The church building was in good repair though not large. Beneath the worship space was a full basement used as auditorium or classrooms. Attached to the church and immediately behind it was a home and offices for the priests. Bishop Fitzgerald had encouraged the establishment of a grade school and that had begun to function in 1946. These classes met in the parish hall beneath the church.

When Bishop Gleeson arrived in 1948, it almost seemed that the people were lying in wait for him. There were ninety-five candidates prepared to receive the Sacrament of Confirmation, and a committee of parents impatient to request permission to construct a grade school. As usual the bishop was introduced at an Episcopal Mass followed by a reception.

The next days were busy with a Confirmation ceremony, visits with military and civilian leaders, and individual and group meetings to discuss possible school building. Before the bishop left on the tenth of October, Bob Slater arrived from Seattle with preliminary plans for a school and six weeks later architectural drawings had been authorized, and bank negotiations were under way.

Now a seasoned traveler the bishop left Fairbanks and arrived in Juneau with over 5000 air miles behind him. One pilot, Oscar Winchel, had flown low enough for him to track bear in their natural habitat near McGrath, and others had flown high enough for him to scan the jumble of mountain peaks and look with awe at smoking craters and miles of pack ice.

Assaulted by the beauty and savagery of the Alaskan scenery, he felt that man had invaded this land before God had finished fashioning it. Many months later he read A Guide to Alaska, Last American Frontier by Merle Colby, and discovered that the evaluation of Alaska he considered wholly original was already in print.

He had visited all the missions with the exception of Nelson Island, and now had enough visual and mental impressions to sort out and think about for the rest of 1948. He also had acquired a great deal of experience in administering the Sacrament of Confirmation. According to the newspaper, The Northwest Progress, he had confirmed more than two hundred adults and children on this first tour.

Another First

One more experience awaited him in November when he attended the United States Catholic Bishops' Conference in Washington, D. C. As was his custom, he listened very intently during the meetings and said little.

Cardinal Amleto G. Cicognani, Papal Delegate, Bishop Gleeson said, *drew me aside for a little chat about Alaska. He asked me if I didn't think it would be appropriate to start dividing up the territory and making another diocese or two up here. I told him that I thought I wasn't sufficiently acquainted with the situation yet to make a judgement.*

Erecting a diocese in Alaska was not a new concept, but one postponed by the death of Bishop Fitzgerald. In replying to the Delegate, Bishop Gleeson asked for and received a year to become better acquainted with his Vicariate.

After the meeting, those bishops who wished financial help customarily attended the Catholic Church Extension Society meeting in Chicago, Illinois. Alaska's bishop certainly wished for financial help; therefore, he went to the meeting. The Extension Society, he heard, was organized to help churches in poor dioceses. He knew that the Vicariate fit the criteria of poor. However, because Alaska was not a diocese, and because it had been entrusted to the care of the Society of Jesus, it did not, strictly speaking, conform to the by-laws of the Extension Society. He also knew that Alaskan priests had been getting stipends from Extension and some of the bishops interested in the missions. Nevertheless, he began to think about other possible alternatives. *These thoughts were interrupted* Gleeson said, *when, His Eminence Cardinal Stritch graciously invited me to say a few words about the needs of the Alaska missions.* Bishop Gleeson's presentation, based on his recent visit around the Vicariate, was vivid and prompted promises of help from the Extension Society, Indian and Negro Missions, the American Board of Catholic Missions, and others. He was elated.

Instead of going straight home at the conclusion of the meeting, the bishop stopped to see friends and relatives in Detroit, and other places. He had never met some of these relatives, and some others he had not seen since he left to become a Jesuit. According to his sister Anna, *it was nice seeing him, but there was little common ground on which to base conversations, so the visit tended to become uncomfortable.* A bit of the problem involved his reluctance to speak hastily on any topic for fear of talking about confidential affairs. It was not until years later, after he retired, that the family truly came to know him a little when he relaxed and communicated with them.

Beginning with this first trip "outside", he made a promise to himself that he would return in time to celebrate the holiday season with his Jesuit brothers. Careful to keep this promise, he could usually be found at home in Alaska from early December until mid-January.

DECISION MAKING: 1949

His rapid swing through the northern Alaska missions, left no doubt that they "were just getting out of the depression;" whereas, the economy in the contiguous states had been in recovery for some years. Overall the slow recovery affected the missions and missionaries more than the average Native people. The resources and funds upon which the missions in Alaska had relied before the depression were cut off or cut down a great deal. One of the results was a general deterioration of the mission buildings and a continuing need for food and clothing for people and clergy alike, especially the children in the schools caring for orphans. Essential teaching materials were in the same short supply as household articles and church linens. Of thirty-three churches, only six were in good condition.

In addition to churches, the Vicariate sponsored schools at Akulurak, Nulato, and Holy Cross. They, too, were in dire need. An Ursuline, Sister Marie Antoinette Johnson, superior at St. Mary's, Akulurak wrote:

The house here, as I write, is shaking like a cradle in the fifty-mile gale. All the buildings are twisting on their foundations this year, even the church which kept straight for so many years. Not only are the sheds parting from this building but one wing is separating from the other and there is an opening of about four inches. The Oregon Jesuit concludes that letter with, *The winds that sweep past Akulurak are ice-honed and potent.*

Throughout his years in administration, Gleeson made a habit of personally gathering all the information available, and then querying advisors, examining precedents, and praying before acting. The pattern served him well and he continued to listen, read, think and pray before speaking.

The First Meeting with Consultors

This year, 1949, the bishop's schedule sent him to the islands south of Juneau to administer the Sacrament of Confirmation. Then, to make his annual retreat, he went to St. Mary's Mission on the Yukon delta on February 7. His Jesuit consultors: Father Provincial Small, Jesuit Superior in Alaska Paul C. Deschout, and Jesuit Fathers Menager, Lonneux, O'Connor, Llorente, Spils, Fox, and Convert were due to meet with him immediately following the retreat.

In addition to the consultors, for the first time in Alaskan history, all other Jesuits from the area were invited to attend. Nine priests and two Brothers came. Their presence and the lively discussions that were a hallmark of Jesuit deliberations afforded the bishop an opportunity to observe the men serving the missions. He saw at firsthand their strong, individual personalities, their willingness to support their beliefs, and their mode of acceptance after a decision had been reached. He was pleased with this opportunity to understand the character of these pastors as well as some of the problems they faced.

About Mission Buildings

Fittingly, said the bishop, *the big discussion for that whole meeting was what to do about Akulurak.* There was no disputing the urgency of the problem; nevertheless, a lively debate ensued. They considered the possibility of moving the children from St. Mary's elsewhere to an established school.

Brother Murphy had been at Akulurak since 1915 and presented some cogent reasons for moving. He said that raising the buildings from their foundations, inserting a series of strong beams and then resetting the structures could stabilize them. This would be very costly because there was no adequate wood for beams on the tundra; consequently, barges would have to ferry in the wood. In addition to cost, ferrying might be impossible because sandbars, leaving a bare eighteen inches of clearance for boats, were closing the Yukon River to commerce.

The Fathers seriously deliberated about building at a new location. A new location would necessitate a builder. Who could be engaged to build? They finally decided that it would be best to build a new school on the Andreafski River. About a hundred miles up the Yukon from Akulurak, this site had been suggested by the late Bishop Fitzgerald. Ground there was firm and free of the permafrost that had ruined so many mission buildings.

By unanimous agreement Father James C. Spils, S.J., commonly addressed as Jake, would be in charge of construction. Reluctantly because of his age and health, the fifty-three year old Jake agreed to build on the condition that Bishop Gleeson would cook for the crew.

The problems at Holy Cross were discussed and temporarily tabled.

Social Issues

Another question on the agenda concerned Jesuit Father Martin J. Lonneux's lifetime work of compiling a dictionary, catechism, and hymn book in Central Yup'ik Eskimo. This monumental task would have been of inestimable value a few years earlier when priests were expected to learn the language of their people. At this time, as Father Fox informed the assembly, the Native population was of a different mind.

At Mountain Village classes in the school and at the other missions were almost doubled in size from the previous year. On All Saints Day, when there was almost a full congregation in the church, a poll of the people was taken to determine the language preferred by them for church services. Surprisingly, everyone including the grandmothers who knew practically no English voted for the greater good of the people to use English. The same thing happened at Marshall where the Eskimo people wanted to learn the language in order to gain status and establish a rapport with white traders and neighbors.

Decision! Bishop Gleeson said that Father Lonneux should purchase a typewriter and any other equipment needed to complete his project.

Another item of great concern to the Fathers of the region was the union activity at the salmon canneries in the Bristol Bay area. The year before, the canning companies had sent a representative to explain what they were offering to the Natives as work conditions and wages, and how their workers would profit from the seasonal work. Most of the priests were skeptical, unwilling to risk Church involvement with social problems.

Here, again, there was spirited debate. Father Endal at Dillingham was anxious that his people get fair wages. Father Convert, who described himself as "some sort of industrial chaplain to the cannery workers," was worried about company employment policies. He was anxious that the Church stand by these vulnerable people as they were introduced to white economic practices. Father Paul C. O'Connor, S.J., whose people traveled from Hooper Bay to Dillingham for the fishing runs, saw a need for their protection in the new environment, and Father Fox from the Yukon villages agreed with him. These four saw the cause as protection of the Natives from exploitation, and from a preliminary move toward political domination. They argued that this was the time and place for the Church to take a stance in the coming dispute.

This, of course, was a delicate subject at that time because of the priests in France and Belgium who shared the life of the working class. There was not a great deal known among the general public about these hundred or so worker priests until their suppression in 1954; however, a number of the missionaries in Alaska came from the countries involved and were well aware of the movement. There was more debate. The mindset of most of those present in Akulurak was that the priests had enough to do to guide their parish people in spiritual matters. The question was tabled for the moment.

Implementation for the Decisions

Finally, satisfied that their efforts were valued and needed changes would move forward, the missionaries left for their assignments. Immediately affected by the meeting was Father Lonneux who left relieved of pastoral duties, and Father Convert who took his place at St. Michael. Sometime after February 27 the bishop and Father Deschout left with Father Convert. Convert was on his way to Kashunak and Father Deschout's people at Tununak were waiting for the bishop to arrive before pulling out for whaling camps on the coast.

Tununak on Nelson Island, was the only mission not visited on the bishop's 1948 trip. Now, in 1949, weather marooned him at Tununak for two weeks during which time he had a cold, hard, uncomfortable dogsled ride, and participated in the departure of the sealing parties. He found that the people were friendly and very devout. A good number of them regularly attended Mass, and other religious services. He was delighted to have the children sing for his Episcopal High Mass.

When favorable weather permitted, he proceeded to an unscheduled stop in Chevak, said to be at the end of nowhere, to Confirm a class of fifty-two people that Father Convert had waiting. Again weather detained him and he walked a bit to become acquainted with the relatively large, muddy Eskimo

117

village. The concentration here of two hundred fifty Eskimos came about as a concession to American Native Services who promised a school if the villages amalgamated.

Father Convert called these people the most backward or childlike of the Natives, but they were farsighted in wanting their children to learn English and better ways of living. So determined were they that they plagued Don C. Foster, General Superintendent of Native Education, for a school as a point of justice since they had fulfilled all the requirements.

It was at Chevak that the bishop became acutely aware that the Natives were interested in learning English and the ways of the white man for a number of reasons. For example: the people were in contact with white officials, the schools their children attended required knowledge of the English language, radios were becoming a part of their way of life, and being able to communicate with white men was a status symbol for them. The bishop encouraged Father to spearhead the demand for a school and that delighted the people, but they were not so happy with their bishop when it was announced that their Father was leaving for Stebbins.

Eventually, the weather moderated and the bishop flew to the area around the Kenai Peninsula for Confirmations. It was at this time that Father Alfred T. Brady, in Juneau as a temporary replacement for Father Conwell, tried, over and over on March 19, to reach Bishop Gleeson at Anchorage, Kodiak, even, Seward, and Sitka. Finally the operator said, The *Bishop is pretty lost right now, isn't he?* If only Father Brady could have known, the bishop had celebrated St. Patrick's Day at Holy Cross Mission.

Before leaving he gave close attention to the condition of the Holy Cross buildings, a subject of discussion at the Akulurak meeting and one bound to resurface in the near future. Along with known urgent needs of updated heating, new equipment, and repairs he saw for himself that docking facilities needed rebuilding to reach the newly receded channel of the Yukon River.

Financial Status of the Vicariate

The multitude of major repairs and immediate improvements were only the visible tip of the many needs. Father O'Connor, Holy Cross Mission Superior, reported the bills for food, clothing and supplies as staggering. His constant prayer was for *a Procurator that would procure for us without having to worry so much about finances.* This, of course, was a futile prayer. The missions had already been supplied for many years with the barest of payments to the suppliers. One vendor, for instance, held a tab for $87,000. Eventually, even the most charitable merchants deemed it necessary to bring suit as a legal insurance of payment. The bishop was keenly aware of these bills and of mission monetary needs. He just had to find a way to solve the cash problem.

In addition to the challenges to his empty coffers, there was a social issue that needed to be addressed. The issue, Native people, especially children, must have exposure to the white culture invading Alaska if scholastic education was to profit them, involved Eskimos and Indians.

Leaving Holy Cross, the bishop made a stop at Andreafski where he scrutinized the claim-stakes driven by Father Llorente in the early spring of 1949 and later adjusted by Father Spils to more stable ground. Satisfied, with the chosen location and the claim stakes the bishop authorized a property description to be sent to Delegate E. L. "Bob" Bartlett for introduction to Congress so that the land could be claimed for use as a mission and building begun.

From Andreafski the Pope's Vicar returned to Juneau where he cleared his desk of letters from priests asking for permissions and organizations inviting him to participate in some celebration or activity. Most importantly during this time he prayed and brooded over the problems presented by his advisors and his missionaries, and the answers he had given.

Decisions with long term consequences for the missions awaited his disposition. In addition to Holy Cross, Father Endal at Dillingham constantly appealed for permission to buy land on which to build a school. To this the answer had to be "No," even though education was a prime concern. Then, too, the socio-economic problems of the Bristol Bay canneries required a more immediate decision than he expected.

He was aware of the French movement allowing priests to hold jobs in the blue-collar workplace. This way of living the Gospel was a form of evangelization seldom practiced by the clergy since the time of Saint Paul. Consequently, Church authorities tended to ignore the situation for a number of years. In spite of the Church policy of turning a blind eye to the Movement, Bishop Gleeson anticipated a change in Church attitudes toward clergy social involvement, and added his support of the Fathers in their union activities to his prayer list.

The Rosary Crusade

Chancellor and bishop had a briefing session before Bishop Gleeson left on April 4 to join the bishops of Alberta and British Columbia on tour to promote the Rosary Crusade popularized by Father Patrick Peyton, C.S.C. After the Crusade, Gleeson boarded a flight to Oregon late in April. The twenty-fifth anniversary for Archbishop Howard provided a short break in the bishop's unflagging pace since the beginning of 1949. He was happy to participate on April 21 in the celebrations for

Edward D. Howard as Archbishop of Portland. Bishop Howard had been a mentor and friend since Gleeson's days as Rector at Sheridan.

Following the celebrations Bishop Gleeson flew to New York for a scheduled meeting of the Marquette League whose members supported the physical needs of the missionaries and their peoples. Many notes in the archives thank this group for their generous contributions of clothing, church linens and other small but necessary items of daily living from shaving equipment to bed linens. He concluded his remarks at their meeting with heartfelt sentiments of appreciation.

Journeying back to Alaska he visited or contacted friends and acquaintances interested in the missions. His last stop on the return was in Ketchikan where, on May 28, he administered the Sacrament of Confirmation. When he finally arrived in Juneau, it had shed its frontier persona. Paved streets had stolen the frontier atmosphere. His stay in Juneau was only to attend to mail and monitor on-going projects.

One of the projects evolved from his having ascertained that Alaska was ready for the erection of a diocese. He realized that such restructuring meant the separation of Jesuit and Vicariate property ownership. To that end, the chancellor had begun the gathering and checking of all Church property surveys and papers of ownership. Coincidentally, Bishop

Gleeson recognized that property in Alaska in the name of the Society of Jesus should be transferred to that of the Vicariate of Alaska. Finally, on June 5 he Confirmed a class at The Nativity of the Blessed Virgin Mary. Then he was again in a plane, this time to Oregon to ordain to the priesthood, Raymond Mosey, his first Vicariate of Alaska candidate.

It was July 19 and time for Bishop Gleeson to substitute for Father O'Flanagan as pastor of Holy Name parish in Anchorage. Working as a parish priest was a wonderful change of pace. The parish work was minimal and left him time for Vicariate correspondence and keeping in touch with the doings of his priests. People often came to the office, but not many like Marie Dorsey (Bronson).

Marie, a public health nurse newly arrived from Baltimore, Maryland, was referred to Anchorage when she telephoned his office in Juneau for an appointment. She had been assigned the Taylor, Richardson and Glenn Highway area abutting Canada on the eastern perimeter. As an active Catholic, Nurse Dorsey was disturbed to find no priest or Catholic chapel in the whole district. Valdez, Anchorage, or Fairbanks was the closest clerical presence in over 300 miles in any direction.

She visited with the bishop at the parish house when she arrived for her appointment. He listened to Nurse Dorsey and recalled that Bishop Coudert of Whitehorse had spoken for the same area in May of 1948. Sitting relaxed in lumberjack shirt and hiking boots, he drew on a cigar and fiddled with his ring for several minutes. Finally, refocusing the hazel eyes he had narrowed in speculation, he turned to his visitor and said that he did have a priest coming up soon. Maybe he would change his assignment and "send him up the highway." Slightly dazed by this prelate's informality as well as the prompt half promise, Marie returned to her duties well impressed by the difference between the formality of Maryland Churchmen and the relaxed reception accorded her by Bishop Gleeson.

A FAR-REACHING DECISION

The priest "coming up soon" was young Father John R. Buchanan, S.J. So it was that Father Buchanan arrived in August of 1949 to find himself offered a 74,000 square mile parish extending from the Beaufort Sea on the north to the border of Valdez on the south, from Canada on the east to the Matanuska Valley on the west. This was a far different assignment from the one he expected as an assistant to the pastor in Dillingham. The offer might have daunted another priest just two years ordained, but husky, enthusiastic Father Buchanan hardly blinked at the challenge. He likes to say that the bishop gave him $5.00 and told him to go do it. His own story, as follows, belies that.

He began work at once to find Tok. Perhaps it is the story of finding any by-way in 1949: *We first found it on a map...but the map didn't have the name "Tok" on it. It only showed a place where the Alcan Highway continued with a road leading south. Then I asked about town where this place was. For the most part it brought only a question on each face until finally I found some who burst out laughing. "Tok!! Wow!!! Sure! I went through there once. Nothing there though. Why?" In a weak, small voice I said, "I'm it."*

Next came transportation. The bishop said a bus went through Tok...also trucks. I asked the laughing ones about it. They laughed some more and said that I had better get some means of personal transportation. I looked for used cars. They were made of gold. I looked at new cars. They were made of taxes. After I had totally given up the idea of being able to get transportation, on a most bright and cheerful day, Father Walsh, the Chaplain here at the Providence Hospital, led me out behind the hospital and showed me a beautiful green Chevrolet pickup. I said, "Whose?" He said, "Yours." I said, "Who?" He said, "Angels." I said, "Which one?" He said, Jack Clawson."

The bishop financed tools, sleeping bag, etc. ...The new district was started. When I left on a late afternoon in late August for Tok, I wondered if the wheels would ever turn. The little car was really sitting back on its haunches. The roads were awful...two hours of mountainous ruts and dust to Palmer and the Matanuska Valley. I was too busy navigating to watch the magnificent scenery around me. Leaving Palmer the sun was setting and the near hills were burning with brilliant color and the mountains were everywhere jabbing into the skies. Then the hurried-closing in of deep black over the vague crags. I bounded along, ate the dust, and late at night arrived at Tazlina Glacier Lodge. When I left there early the next *morning, I had $30 left and fully resolved that Alaskan Lodges were no place to stay unless they would honestly give the stock you had bought in the place to stay the night.*

More mountains and hills and prairies and lakes and color, dust, bumps.

Then I entered my district...Glenn Allenn...a little settlement around the shops and housing of an Alaska Road Commission Camp. It is truly a beautiful setting in the flats, completely surrounded by hills and towering snow-cragged mountains. It was still a hundred and sixty miles to Tok where I was to headquarter, so I continued. But I felt good...I was home. One hundred and sixty miles more of tortuous curves through unspeakably beautiful mountains. Five p.m. found me at the U.S. customs at Tok Junction, on the Alcan Highway, asking for the only Catholic name I knew at Tok – one Jerry Alyn. He was away on vacation. There was a lodge though! I must have paled, though, for Cy Packard then told me that the LaBrees were Catholic. Tok, by the way, sits in absolutely the middle of nowhere. From the south you just suddenly find yourself in the middle of a Road Commission Camp.

I left the Customs and went back to the camp, jumped a little at the sign called "Lodge" and went into the Northern Commercial store to ask directions to the LaBree home. "She just went out the door!" I dashed out and caught up with her.

"Mrs. La Bree?" "Yes." We didn't even slow down. "Catholic Priest. Come in."

Father Buchanan began his whirlwind activities, and the bishop monitored the progress while sitting at his desk perusing letters from other missionaries. One of these letters written by Father Llorente from Bethel gives a fair idea of the type of intelligence coming in on a daily basis. Father wrote:

I banked the Quonset lined it inside with masonite, painted it, finished the wall, and parted it in two. I put an aluminum roofing on the church, built the sidewalk from the road clean to the church, and now I am ready to go upriver and see what can be done there to ameliorate conditions. Don't you just love the word "ameliorate"? While I write to you, I have two Native boys from Keyaluvik painting around me and asking me questions in Eskimo so I am not doing a good job typing. They don't have much initiative and expect me to direct every stroke of the brush.

About one hundred twenty-five Catholics from around King Island are here at present. Last Sunday I gave seventy-five Communions at eight o'clock Mass. The church jammed to the outside door. I think next Spring the church can be enlarged some sixteen feet.

The priests clearly asked the bishop's permission for almost everything they did. Some letters asked for permission to give retreats, to build, and to take vacations. Other letters speak of the missionary traveling to various missions in his 'parish'.

Like a good shepherd the bishop kept an eye on the whereabouts and the doings of all his priests. Except for the visit from Marie and his fulfillment of a priestly assignment to the people in the eastern area of the Territory, daily pastoral duties at Holy Family and for the Vicariate occupied Gleeson for the rest of the summer. Occasionally, parish volunteers released him for short journeys or a day of relaxation. As a token of appreciation for these donated services, he installed a stove in the rectory (O'Flanagan did not cook) and prepared a meal for the volunteers.

Upon Father O'Flanagan's return to Anchorage in August, Bishop Gleeson went to Pilot Station on the tenth for the annual Eskimo Convention. At that same time, some of the girls and Sisters arrived at Andreafski from Akulurak on the thirteenth for a picnic. The girls, brought up in the flat, grey tundra land of the delta, were delighted with the trees and shrubs. They played all around and over the low hills, and picked berries as they walked and talked.

Building Plans for St. Mary's School

The next day, the fourteenth of August, the bishop and Father Fox arrived at Andreafski aboard the Sifton. After Mass on the fifteenth, the bishop, Mother Antoinette, Father Spils and Father Fox discussed building plans for the proposed St. Mary's School.

Completing his consultations at Andreafski he joined the Canadian prelates who had invited him on the Rosary Crusade to visit population centers throughout Alaska. Their schedule took them across the territory from Nome to Anchorage and Adak to Palmer. Their tour then flew to cities in Canada. There was a one-day visit in Juneau on September 25. Then Bishop Gleeson and Archbishop O'Neill of Regina, Saskatchewan, Canada continued by Alaska Coastal for Sitka. Each stop at a parish included the praying of the rosary, a homily, and a solemn Benediction.

Bishop Gleeson did not return to Juneau until October 11 when he arrived aboard the SS Aleutian after Confirming in Wrangell and Petersburg. Some amusing incidents that became often told stories occurred on the tour. For example, at one point Bishop Gleeson touched base with his office in Juneau; the pastor, Robert L. Whelan, rushed into a lengthy report. When he stopped for breath, the operator politely announced that the other user had hung up.

Not all the stories involved humor. After a well-received Crusade visit at the Adak military base, the chaplain arranged a return by plane for the clergymen. Approaching the mainland the plane began changing altitude over the mountains. The men could understand climbing, but when the plane lost height and dodged between mountain peaks, they became a little tense. Quietly they questioned a crewman who explained that the pilot was unsuccessfully endeavoring to de-ice the wings. He did not have to explain that there was, in fact, imminent danger of crashing into a ridge directly before them. For a moment a large lake appeared just beyond the ridge. If only the pilot could raise the sagging plane! Anxious minutes and expert flying coaxed the plane up and over to where it could sink and circle until the warmer lake air melted the ice and it dropped away. They all agreed that flying is not for the faint hearted.

Alaska Ready for a Diocese

The Crusade tour concluded Bishop Gleeson packed his bags for the annual meeting in Washington. As promised he met with Papal Delegate Cicognani and gave as his opinion that Southeastern Alaska was indeed ready to become an independent diocese; thus, he set the wheels turning in Rome. From Washington he traveled to Chicago for the Extension Society meeting where he was assured of continued help from Extension, the Indian and Negro Missions, the Catholic Mission Society, and several individuals.

His aim to rehabilitate three or four missions a year began to look possible. Usually the stipend from the various societies paid for shipping of needed building supplies, anywhere from ten thousand to twenty thousand dollars for each church building. Other sources provided interior needs such as altar, candles, stations, linens, and so forth.

Included on the homeward trip was a stop in Seattle where the bishop met with architect Arthur T. Kane concerning the building of St. Mary's at Andreafski. Mr. Kane, a Jewish friend of Father Spils, proved to be an extremely kind and generous man. When it came time to talk contract and payment he put the lights and tinsel on Bishop Gleeson's Christmas tree by volunteering his time and expertise for plans and architectural advice. The holiday season with his brother Jesuits in Juneau was shared with joy.

Building Underway: 1950

In early January Father Endal was taking advantage of an unusually warm winter and building his long sought after school in Dillingham. With the prospect of a school he began begging the bishop for Sisters to staff the school and priests to help him in the parish. He was looking especially for someone knowledgeable in the Russian Orthodox Rite. Father Buchanan might have been the man Father Endal would have welcomed except that he was destined for other work.

Next to Buchanan, Father Endal was anxious to have as his assistant Father George T. Boileau, S.J., former cook at Sheridan's building site. Father Endal may have requested Father Boileau; however, changes only took place when the Superior of the Jesuits in Alaska was convinced of a need, recognized the required talents in a certain priest, and had his placement authorized by the bishop. The bishop had the last word in the placement of priests. Indeed, his word prevailed in all matters concerning the Vicariate. In this case the bishop went to Seattle, and Boileau did not become Endal's assistant.

When Bishop Gleeson went to Seattle, Father Spils came from Alma and met him at Arthur Kane's office where the three men worked on plans for St. Mary's. They labored during the remainder of January and most of February preparing for the proposed building. Arthur Kane drew up the architectural plans, and Father Spils, using the skills he had learned as a boy and honed to excellence as he worked on the missions, estimated structural materials to within seven window frames and one bag of cement. Specification changes made during work on the building accounted for miscalculations.

While Father Jake Spils and Art Kane performed math magic, the bishop ordered a cooking range, kitchenware and foodstuffs for the nourishment of eight to twenty-three men working from June to the full onset of winter in October. Gleeson and Spils together bought a small John Deere tractor, digging machines, and lumber. Their combined purchases had a transportation fee of more than $20,000. Both the bishop and the supplying companies had more than their share of faith. In fact, the bishop had some second thoughts when he saw the bills, but one of the priests told him that if he began the money would be there. He must have lived the rest of his life on that belief.

While preparations for St. Mary's progressed in Seattle, the people of Immaculate Conception parish in Fairbanks struggled with first steps toward erecting an elementary school. Father Anable, their pastor, flew to Seattle late in January to borrow money for construction. His task was tantamount to asking for a miracle because banks everywhere shied away from lending where the economy seemed so unstable. When Father returned in March, he reported his lack of success to Bishop Gleeson who conferred with financial advisors. On their advice he transferred the land for the school building from the diocese to the parish as a corporate sole on March 19. In the end, obtaining the bank loan took longer than the construction of the elementary school.

The planning and discussion taking place in Seattle and Fairbanks was being matched on the missions engaged in building or repairing activities. A letter came to Chancellor Conwell, the bishop's alter ego in Juneau, in which Father Donohue said that he is spending the winter with his people in New Knock Hock as much as possible while he is completing work on their new church. Later he received checks from the Extension Society and the Indian Mission Society paying for the construction and furnishings of the new building. The next month Donohue wrote to Father Conwell,

Don't you sometimes yearn for a place at one of these quiet missions where the priests have nothing to do but study Lingua Eskimo? Well, don't ever give in to such an idea. The above is as far as I got March 5; that's just the heading, and today, March 31, is my first chance since. Got home from a tour of the Yukon day before yesterday; had to leave at 8 p.m. on a sick call in a different direction; returned late yesterday afternoon; leave tomorrow morning for Holy Week at New Knock Hock.

Returned from Seattle, Bishop Gleeson had the opportunity to inspect the new churches being constructed in the bush as he continued his annual round of the Vicariate. His visits elicited many different reactions from the priests. Father Llorente says of the bishop's travels:

He would live with the priest wherever he went. These were very primitive dwellings. I (Segundo Llorente) was weather-bound with him several times in the bush. He would sit very quietly listening to my constant chatting. In Bethel, while he sat in the kitchen, I walked up and down the floor giving him my humble opinion on all sorts of mission problems. I was very careful to say always "MY HUMBLE OPINION" until he got fed up and when I came out with another humble opinion he interrupted me to say, "Humble but FIRM." He was witty as they come; sharp as a razor.

Sharp wit is likely to be a bit cruel. Some priests definitely did not appreciate the bishop's wit. Of course, sometimes the listener accepted it as hilarious despite the intent of the storyteller. It was easy to find examples of his witty remarks and just as easy to understand them as cruel or funny often depending upon how one felt on a particular day.

Ready in May for a vacation from his travels, the bishop demonstrated his satisfaction with his pastoral break at Anchorage by offering to substitute as pastor in Cordova while Father David Melbourne took a two-week holiday. There is no evidence of important decisions having been made during this time; it was just a pleasant change for both clergymen. Afterward Bishop Gleeson was refreshed and ready for the cooking stint he had accepted as his part in the construction of St. Mary's. On his way to Andreafski, he stopped in Fairbanks to bless, on June 1, the opening of the new wing of St. Joseph's Hospital administered by the Sisters of Providence.

Gleeson the Cook

From Fairbanks he proceeded to the Andreafski building site. Stepping off the plane at five-thirty on the evening of June 8, he announced to an ailing Father Spils, his two nephews, and four young men from Holy Cross that he had seen the Nenana barge near Marshall and that it should be in about six. Jake Spils and his men had arrived four days earlier to ready a landing site for the barge and to prepare a space for its cargo.

As soon as the barge tied up, the young men unloaded the tons of freight. The long arctic day allowed them full light and they finished by ten o'clock. The next day fifteen workers came from Pitkas Point to provide a double construction crew on six-hour shifts. Thanks to the bishop regular meals, prepared on a Yukon camp stove, appeared every mealtime.

Unprotected from an onslaught of rain and high wind, the crews sloshed through mud and could make little headway in building. Six sets of rain gear arrived by barge on the tenth affording the workers a little protection. A cooking range came in that shipment, but, except for the cooking room it afforded, the stove helped very little because supplies were buried amid tons of materials piled before the camp. Cook Gleeson made do with fresh fish and a barrel each of salt pork and beef.

Confined to the cookhouse, he cut his hair in such a shaggy manner that Father Jake called attention to it and claimed it proof positive that the bishop would stay the summer. At this sally, the laymen were impressed but the bishop merely smiled. He knew that he was there for emergency decisions and cooking was simply an excuse. A boy helped with odds and ends and washed dishes. Everyone concurs that the crew ate royally. Vegetables and extra cuts of caribou, and fowl came at intervals from Holy Cross. They also supplied clean laundry and fresh bread. Except for Sundays and feast days that were for rest and relaxation, construction activity was strenuous and unremitting. For the bishop there was cooking and the solving of problems, perhaps more accurately, the listening to problems.

On June 20 Fathers Convert and Endal came to consult with him about union difficulties, and shortly thereafter Bishop Gleeson received an anguished letter from Bjorne Halling, International Union Representative, asking for an appointment. The bishop agreed to see the Union man on July 15; however, when Halling arrived the bishop allowed him to unburden himself regarding the doings of Convert and Endal in their unprecedented interference in the fishing industry, and then, as only the bishop could, responded with, *Mmmmm.* It was hardly the answer Halling wanted. He left, free to interpret as he chose.

Four days later the bishop traveled to Fairbanks to ready himself for a flight to Seattle. He was delighted to be included in the July 21 ceremonies for the ordination of Father Joseph Dougherty as Bishop of Yakima, a newly created diocese. Yakima had continued to grow since Francis left more than thirty years before.

After the ordination and attendant festivities, the bishop returned to Alaska to spend the feast of St. Ignatius, July 31, at Akulurak with the priests from Holy Cross and St. Mary's. Four days later a group of priests traveled to Nulato to celebrate the seventy-fifth anniversary of the founding of the Nulato mission. From Nulato the bishop went to Hooper Bay to transfer some

Church property into Native hands and then hurried back to Andreafski to confer with Sister Philippa from Akulurak about extensive changes in the blue prints, changes that ultimately necessitated extra windows and delayed construction. An exasperated Spils was heard to grumble, *It seems a rabbit warren is desired.*

St. Mary's at Akulurak

St. Mary's Mission at Akulurak had been in continuous operation since 1905. During those years, orphans and children too young to help the hunter-gatherer families were left under the care of the Jesuits and the Ursuline Sisters. Primarily, the role of the school was to shelter and give whatever indoctrination possible in a few years. The children were taught the rudiments of the English language, reading, personal hygiene, preservation of food and survival with an emphasis on Christian living. With the new school, the Sisters hoped to concentrate on academics and prepare the children for a place in business or scholastic society. They wanted this to be a school to teach the young people how to compete in a world of the white man's language and customs. Bishop Gleeson applauded this concept.

As June had welcomed the bishop with rain and wind, September saw him off with more of the same. Watching the men lift a section of the roof into place, he remarked, *This place is almost as rainy as Juneau.* He then turned in his apron and resumed his visitation schedule, going first to Mountain Village for the Eskimo Convention and later to Seattle for its Centennial celebration.

Father Tom and the Army

While in Seattle the bishop spoke with Father Small about Father Thomas A. Cunningham, recently pastor at Nome. "Father Tom," as he was popularly known had taken his physical in July, ostensibly to fulfill his two-month military reserve training. Cunningham was eager for an army hitch and the army was eager to have him. It was the Geophysical Year. The military services were studying the Arctic ice floes and Father had unique talents for recognizing the stress capabilities of a flat mass of floating ice. This knowledge was vital to the air rescue operations in northern climates. After listening to military superiors explain their need for Father Tom's special talent, the bishop released Father for duty. In Seattle Father Provincial heard the reasons for Father Tom's release for military service.

Giving a priest to the Army was a real deprivation for the missions. A second deprivation surfaced in October when the Catholic Mission Knitting Society, an arm of the Propagation of the Faith, notified the bishop that they were ceasing activities. For more than thirty years they had donated annually over a thousand pieces of warm clothing for both priests and people in Alaska. The loss of their help was cause for great sadness.

At times like this his busy schedule was some help. He came back to Juneau from the Seattle Centennial celebrations and began packing for the November meeting of Bishops. This entailed more than a change of clothing in a suitcase because this time he would be returning to Fairbanks. He had reported to the Holy See in 1949 that he believed it was time for a diocese to be formed in the southeastern area of the Territory of Alaska. Given a year to let the wheels turn in Rome, Bishop Gleeson calculated that the new diocese would soon be announced; hence, his decision to move his headquarters for the Vicariate of Alaska to Fairbanks.

He would leave Father Conwell in Juneau to mentor the new bishop. That being so, before leaving for the Bishops' Conference and the Extension meeting he had to brief Father Conwell on his double role as mentor in Juneau and chancellor to the Vicariate of Northern Alaska. Only then could he pack to ship his belongings to Fairbanks.

THE UNIONS AND THE ALASKA NATIVES

A Continuing Dispute

The visit from Bjorne Halling in July of 1950 was not the beginning of Fishermen vs. Unions and Big Business in Alaska, but Bishop Gleeson's "Mmm" for the union man was the beginning of the bishop's serious consideration of the missioners concerns. The troubles began well before Bishop Gleeson arrived in Juneau. However, when the missioners became fully aware that the unions were biased in favor of industry and that the Communist ideology might influence the Native workers, the Church and the bishop were called upon to act according to the Gospel message.

In his position as Papal Vicar, Bishop Gleeson was always careful to follow Papal intentions. In this instance the bishop was keenly aware of the Papal instructions for priests to avoid all but spiritual instruction/explanation; nevertheless, he believed the Church needed to help the people resolve this union problem.

In Alaska the bishop took the initial steps in the change from solely spiritual help by priests, to help in the everyday living of the Gospel, by allowing the missioners to lend their knowledge and support to the workers in the fishing industry. A brief account of the bishop's quiet supportive permission as attested to by Fathers Convert and Endal follows.

Father Convert said, *With the Bishop's consent, for the 1950 season, I went back as a worker so I'd have the right to take the floor at any organizational meeting.* Father soon discovered that Harry Bridges union had a contract with the companies. To frustrate Bridge's organizers, Father Convert immediately scurried around explaining to the Native workers why they should not accept the offered contract. Consequently, as soon as the supply ships departed Seattle ports so that work could not be held up, workers signed an amended contract with Father Convert as their Union Organizer and Representative. Later Father said he heard that Bridges wrote to Bishop Gleeson (1950) *complaining, that I was a tool of the Companies and a union-buster.* The bishop requested that Father Convert answer these charges. Father immediately submitted a line by line refutation and from that the bishop drew his own conclusion.

There were eight unions involved, and when Father Convert's cannery workers union and Bridge's union for the fishermen could not reach a common ground, it meant complicated bargaining for the canning companies. As a consequence, in 1951, the canning companies refused to negotiate separate contracts, and both unions went on strike. Bosses, office and kitchen workers processed fish until farm workers from California could be imported for the canning season.

The Bristol Bay fishing problems came into prominence again in September 1951 when Father Endal with three other Union Committeemen put out a brief statement spotlighting one of the basic reasons Seattle business worked so hard to deprive Alaska of statehood. These reasons appeared in <u>The Oregon Jesuit</u> in November 1952:

The fundamental problem was to bring about such conditions as will leave more of the great wealth now taken out of Alaska annually. The Salmon pack of Bristol Bay is valued at from $15,000,000 to $40,000,000. Less than 10% of this stays in the district.

The proposed solution:

1. *Resident ownership of fishing equipment.*
2. *Abandonment of the Fish and Wildfire Service in favor of the Territorial Department of Fisheries.*
3. *Definite limitation of fishing effort with preference to residents.*

It was at this crisis, Father Convert believes, that the bishop really put his reputation on the line when he backed his priests before industrialists of the Northwest United States. "Good Catholics" of the industry diplomatically asked the bishop if he knew what one of his young priests was doing in Bristol Bay, to which the answer was a firm affirmation. Then the same fellows or their bosses appealed to the Archbishops of Seattle and San Francisco, who transmitted the accusations to Rome, who passed it routinely to our Father General, who routinely also requested the Oregon Provincial to furnish a report on the affair.

Father Clifford A. Carroll, S.J., the socio-economics professor at Gonzaga University and active in labor conciliation, was asked to investigate and submit a very thorough report in 1951. A bit later Father Convert received a message from Father General encouraging him to continue. The bishop's message from the Father General came through a visit from Father Carroll who congratulated him warmly for the work of the priests on this matter.

Alarmed at the chaotic turn of events and true to their conviction that the Church should stay out of social problems, some of the Jesuits scolded Father Convert in no uncertain terms. When Convert asked Bishop Gleeson where he had been imprudent thus deserving of censure by other Jesuits, Father said, *I can still see him in his rocking chair, quietly grumbling and finally coming with a final verdict: "Prudence is a gift of the*

Spirit, sure, but so is Fortitude." And that's all he ever said to me about the whole affair.

The National Labor Relations Board, after many appeals by Father Convert, made an inquiry and condemned the Industry, reinstating fired workers without loss of seniority, but ruling that a civil court would have to settle compensation. For Convert to go to court, he would have to have Bishop Gleeson's approval. About the visit to seek approval, he wrote,

Then I could go to Fairbanks to make my presentation to Bishop Gleeson who just grunted his approval (I guess), but asked me exactly what I had asked from the NLRB, what about compensation; so I told him that would be a new business in court and he just mentioned very casually that I better get the wheels turning right then.

In a letter in 1977, Jules Convert wrote: *I rather believe that what I did then with Father Endal of Dillingham marked the beginning of the Mission's concern in the human condition of the Natives and activity in socio-economic affairs; marked also the first time that the Natives of Northwest Alaska came together for a joint action.*

As Father Convert noted, the union strife around Dillingham united the Native people in the workplace. Pressured by the canning companies to bypass the unions and sign individual contracts, they heeded a Unalakleet man who said in substance, *We are united for the first time without any regard to our different religious affiliations. We have an able Alaskan leadership of our own choice. We should go home together and stick together.* Father Convert wrote proudly of them, *Last week has made men out of our 'Boys' and I am proud of the stand they freely adopted.*

By turning down the offers, the Native men sacrificed winter security, but built within themselves a new pride. This was the kind of maturity the bishop hoped his priests could help their people achieve. It prompted him to return more Church property to the Native community, and to hope that they might begin offering themselves for a Native Priesthood.

A Jules Convert Insight

Several Jesuits commented on the bishop's noncommittal grunt that Convert interpreted as approval. These are Convert's insights:

Some reproached him (Biship Gleeson) with this apparent lack of leadership; it came in part that he is an extremely prudent man and as such tends to procrastinate, often waiting to the last minute to make decisions under the pressure of circumstances when he has to make his move and is then quite assured it is the right one; until then, he leaves full freedom to the 'man on the spot' who knows better all the detailed circumstances. This contributed to make him an excellent Superior, but you had to get first to know his way. But he was certainly the type who wants to keep in his hands all the reins, who feels the need to continually watch over the shoulders of those under him.

Father Francis J. Fallert, S.J., extended the bishop's "Mmmm" to the look that accompanied the sound. The two actions plus one's own good conscience dictated the interpretation according to Father Fallert.

The union infighting obviously claimed some of the bishop's attention; but did not seriously impede Vicariate duties. As he visited the various missions during July and August, bishop and missionaries shared thoughts about the omnipresent union problems and the associated political issue of the statehood of Alaska.

In 1940 the appraised value of the physical properties of the mining and canning industries was estimated at more than a half-billion dollars. The fish pack in 1946 was $56,571,000 and the territorial tax $630,000. Because cannery operators feared state control of the fisheries and the abolition of fish traps, it is not too difficult to understand why, in 1950, the Seattle-based salmon industry fought fiercely against statehood for Alaska. With its intense determination and large organization it is equally easy to understand why the bill for statehood was defeated. These were the white man's issues about which priests strove to educate their people.

THE VICAR MOVES TO FAIRBANKS: 1951

Both the Washington and Chicago meetings were routine; as a consequence the bishop arrived in Fairbanks by December 6. There he found Father Boileau helping with parish duties at Immaculate Conception, so Gleeson unpacked and brought himself up-to-date on Vicariate business. As a New Year surprise for the Catholics of Fairbanks he celebrated a High Mass at the midnight holy hour followed by his Episcopal Mass at midnight.

After the holidays, the people surprised the bishop by their active interest in politics. From the military bases to the Native villages people were discussing the congressional debates concerning the care and disposition of Native Americans in Alaska. This had been a political item for several years, but it claimed special attention at this time because everyone, especially the missionaries and military were aware of the invaluable service Alaskan Native people had rendered during World War II.

Territorial Governor Ernest Gruening spoke vehemently against Native reservations. His views were widely circulated through the press. Outside of Alaska Monsignor John B. Tennelly, head of the Negro and Indian Mission Society, expressed concern that some lawyers with self-interests were misleading the Alaskan Natives. He believed in reservations, as did Father Hubbard of Alaskan exploration and lecture renown.

Priests and people in the isolation of the bush were uncertain about the politics of the issues. Father Donohue, in his role as Superior of the missionaries, asked Father Conwell for information, and for explanations of any stand the Church might have taken in the matter. Father had no answer for him. There were no precedents for Bishop Gleeson to study except the reservations in the contiguous states. Having administered the school in Omak, Washington, he had observed an Indian reservation at firsthand; however, he did not consider his experience as solid expertise on which to rely. He knew that, in general, the Alaskan Natives were against statehood and the reservation proposals before Congress. He suspected they were not fully informed on the pros and cons of the political ramifications.

Bishop Gleeson, himself, inclined always toward trusting the person most concerned to handle himself best if given freedom to do so. On the question of reservations he kept his own counsel. In doing so, he allowed his priests to discuss with their people, in a non-teaching capacity, the pros and cons of reservations. In the end, many of the Eskimo and Indian people alike came to the conclusion that reservations were not in store for them and it was safe for them to favor statehood.

Statehood, too, was not a new political issue. A relatively small group of industrialists with economic and political machinations kept this huge land mass as a Territory. Now that the army had constructed the Alaskan Highway and commercial air transport was viable, the residents of the Territory began an active campaign for statehood. This and three other considerations moved Congress to rethink Territorial demands for statehood. The three factors: 1. The military presence from Second World War doubled the population of the Territory. 2. The participation of the Native population in defending their land in Alaska for the United States. 3. Alaska's worth as a military buffer zone between East and West. Bishop Gleeson was cognizant of all these issues; however, as a Bishop, he was careful to maintain the separation of Church and State in his public speech.

During these first months of 1951, he listened in Fairbanks and took the opportunity to visit surrounding areas. One of his visits took him to the village of Nenana. Nenana, a railway and barge stop some fifty miles southwest of Fairbanks, was once a large community of railway workers who left when the tracks were laid. A tiny group of people, mostly non-Catholic, remained, and eventually no priest visited Nenana. During the weeks before Bishop Gleeson's installation the Church property was put up for sale. When a possible buyer backed out and there was no other offer, the bishop looked at the church building and decided that he would attempt to serve the needs of the Catholics who lived in the village.

Nenana Has a Pastor

Soon he began to say a Sunday Mass in Fairbanks and then take the train to Nenana to say another Mass there. Among the parish activities he performed in Fairbanks were visits to the sick, counseling those who came to him, administering the sacraments, and encouraging lay participation in parish activities. Under his direction and mentoring a group formed an Altar Society.

In Nenana, he did many of the same things, and he showed a unique kindness to the children. After saying Mass there, visitors noticed that no one left the church until the bishop removed his vestments and came down the aisle to greet the people. He invariably gave each child a candy bar. This was not by way of a bribe to bring them to Mass, but his way of alleviating a bit of their poverty. In addition, in Nenana, rather than promoting an Altar Society, he assumed the duties of caretaker. His next door neighbors, not Catholic, saw him sweeping and tidying around the property whenever he was in residence.

He seldom appeared in Episcopal cassock and cross except when he said Mass. Then, whether it was a private or public liturgy, he always wore his Episcopal insignias. After his daily private Mass, he would prepare breakfast for himself and his priest-server. Following is a typical breakfast scene as described by Father Wilfred P. Schoenberg, S.J.

He went to the kitchen, and still wearing his Bishop's robes, he got the breakfast. He had everything lined up. He'd put the bacon in the oven, there'd be the coffee, and there he'd be standing with his big "pot" and his great big cincture, turning over the eggs, taking the toast out, and he didn't want me to interfere. Father Scheonberg delighted in teasing the bishop about his weight.

Lent in 1951 began in February and in Fairbanks every Wednesday evening the bishop taught a mini-series on the Holy Sacrifice of the Mass and Father Boileau augmented the series at Sunday Mass. The bishop then returned to Nenana to resume his pastoral duties there. By Laetare Sunday Father Boileau was in the hospital with the flu, and upon his return to duty, the bishop came down with the virus. The mini-series was discontinued until after Easter.

Those weeks of commuting between village and city convinced the bishop that he could conduct Church business as well from Nenana as from Fairbanks. Consequently, during that Lent, he sent to Holy Cross for Jesuit Brother John Hess to help him renovate the Nenana church and priest's quarters. Brother and bishop worked fairly steadily on the renovations until March 18 when the bishop officiated in Fairbanks at the dedication of the new wing of St. Joseph's Hospital which stood just behind the Immaculate Conception church and belonged to the Sisters of Providence. The same community of Sisters also staffed Immaculate Conception School.

Everyone from news media to visitors from surrounding communities praised the new wing and its modern equipment. Because this was the only medical facility in the city, the general public was thrilled with the improvements. In a quid pro quo arrangement the hospital Sisters extended hospitality to the bishop and visiting clergy whenever there was need, and served three meals a day to the parish priests. In return, the priests, and often the bishop, attended to the chaplain' duties.

By Easter time Bishop Gleeson returned to Nenana where he continued to work with Brother Hess on the repairs to the St. Theresa Church building. Anyone wishing to see him had to make a long trip by automobile over a scenic, slow and hazardous road, or by Alaska Railroad, an equally slow and scenic route. On one occasion a group of Sisters of Providence drove down to visit the bishop at Nenana. The approach to the village necessitated crossing the Tanana River where there was no bridge and they were terrified because the ice was so clear they could see the rushing waters below.

Once across, their car slid into a snowdrift where they sat helpless until rescued by some passing Indian men, who, without uttering a single word, picked up the car and put it back on the roadway. Trembling from cold and bewilderment, the Sisters reached the bishop's residence where they managed to regain their poise as they visited and shared a picnic lunch with the bishop. It was an adventurous day, and they had yet to brave the return trip through the foothills between Nenana and Fairbanks.

Early in the next month, May 1951, Father Donohue wrote a letter to Father Conwell asking if the Catholic students of Bethel should attend the graduation ceremonies from the school since the ceremonies would be held in the Moravian Church. Attendance would make the Catholics look like second class citizens. This had long been a bone of contention. There was no other place to hold the ceremonies so Father was advised to resolve the issue peacefully.

If the graduation problem seems miniscule, the proposition Father Anable presented to the bishop when he returned to

Nenana from a mission tour was of major importance. Father suggested that a barge be built to house a fish cannery. It should stand on the Andreafski River fronting on school property. He reasoned that canning promised to be more efficient than salting for the ten thousand or more fish required each year to serve the St. Mary's School faculty, staff and boarders. The cannery would also preserve fish sticks for sale to local people. The bishop promised to think about it.

In the meantime Gleeson boarded the train for Fairbanks where he was scheduled to conduct a Confirmation ceremony on May 13. The military chaplains came to help with the liturgical requirements. Afterward the bishop quickly returned to Nenana and his refurbishing work where he and Brother were joined for a week in July by John J. Wood, S.J., a newly ordained man on the Alaska missions and a possessor of precision building skills.

During July the bishop also took time to meet with Father Anable (The acting pastor changed frequently) and the people interested in the Fairbanks schools to consider ways and means to raise money. At first they considered a bazaar, but bazaars usually did not raise as much money as their project would cost. They finally opted for a cash appeal.

Meanwhile, letters from Father Llorente throw some light on the progress being made at Andreafski and its impact on

Akulurak as well as bush ways of obtaining money. Father Llorente's first letter contains this description: *New Knock Hock is the south end of my new 5,000 square mile quasi parish. It must be about sixty-five miles from here (Akulurak), I guess. Akulurak will remain as a village of some nine families. It may die eventually or it may increase to unsuspected proportions.* The following month he adds this snippet to the coastal picture, *My Akulurak church is finished, 18x38. The old rectory has been tampered with and it is now a lovely chateau 16x24 with an ideal view.* And another letter sheds some financial information:

Father Anable, at Akulurak did well with the salmon strips. He should turn well over $5,000 to his Excellency. Akularak is scheduled to move en masse on July 15...I plan to be there to kiss them all goodbye.

At the time Catholics in the city of Fairbanks prepared to build, most of the villagers at Akulurak prepared to move into quarters near the new school, and Bishop Gleeson at Nenana, prepared to go to Andreafski for the opening of St. Mary's School. In the midst of his preparations a letter arrived on July 13 from Apostolic Delegate Archbishop Cicognani. Its announcement was of even greater consequence for the Catholic Church in Alaska than the new schools for which so many people prepared. In part the letter said,

I have received word from the Holy See that publication will be made on Wednesday, July 18th, of the erection of the new Diocese of Juneau with the Reverend Robert D. O'Flanagan as First Bishop. We shall make the usual announcement here to the Press Services, but in the meanwhile I ask Your Excellency to apprise Father O'Flanagan of the date of publication.

Until such time as the new Bishop takes possession of his See, Your Excellency will be Apostolic Administrator of the New Diocese.

Although the announcement of a new diocese had been expected it came at a particularly busy time and the bishop had no opportunity to dwell on the effect the loss of the most financially sound part of his Vicariate would have on the Church in northern Alaska.

His appointment as Apostolic Administrator posed no problem. After all, since the beginning of the year, he had been residing in Fairbanks and Nenana and transacting business for the Church in southern Alaska through his Chancellor in Juneau. The announcement did cause excitement for Father O'Flanagan.

TWENTY-FIVE YEARS AS A PRIEST

Chaplains Woodrow L. Elias from Ladd Field and Clement Shaughnessy of the Eielson Air Force base tried several times to make an appointment with Bishop Gleeson and finally managed to see him on July 24. Their aim was to relieve his heavy schedule with a little humor. Very solemnly they each presented him with a box of cigars. They said that it was in the hope that two of these regular size cigars will equal one of the Roman Candle type you so magnificently extend. The ruse elicited a deep rumbling chuckle that was the bishop's way of laughing. He waved them to chairs in his office and they began making basic arrangements for a Solemn Pontifical Mass on July 29 in Immaculate Conception Church. They meant this to be the beginning of a joyous celebration for Bishop Gleeson's twenty-five years in the priesthood.

Priests and lay people, Catholic and non-Catholic, family, and friends from Fairbanks, surrounding villages, towns, military installations, and the northwestern contiguous states, received invitations. People came from everywhere before and during the festivities on the twenty-ninth. It seemed that God was trying to compensate for the paucity of visitors on his ordination day in Spain.

The Blessing of St. Mary's School

His jubilee celebrations barely over, he traveled to St. Mary's to bless the new school. The Oregon Jesuit published the following descriptions of the move from Akulurak to Andreafski. First a description by Brother Robert Benish:

After much waiting for freight, barges did not get to Marshall till about the 25th of July, the Sifton arrived with the Holy Cross and George Shepherd's barges on July 31, the feast of St. Ignatius.

We went to work with gusto right away, loading up. And Thursday noon got underway. About 9:30 both barges were full and Brother Alfred Murphy, said only essentials should come, well Sisters had lots of essentials. Anyway, we finally got underway with a full load: 115 children, 3 Sisters, Father Menager, Brother Murphy, myself and the dogs—and the essentials.

We made fish camp by 8 o'clock, slept overnight, got up at 4:30, had Mass—First Friday—at 5 o'clock, got underway again at 6:30—arrived at Andreafski at 9:45. The weather was beautiful. Brother Murphy will go back for another two barge-loads tomorrow, August 7.

Sister George Edmond of Holy Cross writes this account of the bishop's trip to Andreafski:

Bishop Gleeson and Father William McIntyre, S.J., were also passengers on Jim Walker's boat. The Bishop and Father slept in Father John Fox's cabin while the rest of us caught forty winks on the boat that first night en route.

After two days of travel we reached Andreafski at 7:30 p.m. What a wonderful reception awaited us there! The Pilgrim Statue of Fatima had preceded us by a few hours only. Father Fox's convention was underway and the great number of boats gave one the impression of a large city dock—except for the mud.

Wish you could see the beautiful building Father put up at Andreafski. From the river it looks like a grand white palace. I had thought the aluminum siding would make it look like a warehouse, but it doesn't...it looks like white paint...And then the marvel of Andreafski: the chapel. Every bit of it is a prayer. The sanctuary is done in plywood paneling....Father James Spils, did a work of art in placing the grain—the light panel with the darker strip forming the shadow.

The feast day of the Assumption of Mary on August 15 and the blessing of the school coincided with the conclusion of a three-day round-the-clock recitation of the rosary to honor the presence of the traveling statue of the Virgin Mary of Fatima. The ceremonies concluded with the Sisters providing a feast for builders and clergy. It was a spectacular celebration for so small a community, especially one in the process of moving into new buildings. The buildings had no finishing work done, and most of the furnishings stood in packing crates. Providing housing and a banquet for those present leaves one amazed at the Sisters' ingenuity.

The New St. Mary's Mission

This first major building project, St. Mary's Mission on the Andreafski River, undertaken by the last Vicar Apostolic of all of Alaska had its location suggested by Bishop Fitzgerald and confirmed by his successor Bishop Gleeson in 1950. In 1951 the school opened its doors to the children of the old St. Mary's, Boarding School at Akulurak. In 1952 a high school program was initiated, providing education and boarding facilities for grades one through twelve for children of the surrounding villages and towns. By 1974 St. Mary's had become solely a secondary school program, a combination day and boarding school serving grades nine through twelve. It enjoyed a statewide reputation as an outstanding educational institution that prepared its students for social integration either at home or in a wider community. Its graduates were ready to enter into a school of their choice for higher education. The 1950 dreams of the Sisters and of Bishop Gleeson were in full flower.

When the celebrations for the opening of St. Mary's concluded, the bishop went on to Nome to continue visitations until August 29 when he returned to Nenana. He was anxious to finish his living quarters so that he could send for his personal belongings.

That same month saw a flurry of letter writing between the procurator in Seattle and the bishop's office. There had been an unwritten understanding that potentially useful items, such as paint and small machinery, might be procured for the missions when they became available at a good price. Because these were days of tight budgeting in the Vicariate, the procurator was given notice that the bishop did not wish to be billed for any items not ordered through his office. This notification was not appreciated in the Seattle office, and missionaries were dismayed when they were told to look for second hand generators or other articles rather than the new fittings they needed.

Some of the men sent rather bitter messages concerning the ruling, and at least one missionary received a letter from the chancellor saying that the bishop was paying his bill with great reluctance. The Fathers were also reminded that a great deal of money had been expended on the building of St. Mary's. It was suggested that a "good buy" be queried as to need either at a particular mission or at the mission warehouse.

The building program was taking on a new meaning for the men in the field and those attempting to supply their needs.

Another unusual communication from the bishop was a telegram of good wishes to Father Dave McAstocker for his Golden Jubilee. Up until this time, the bishop had made a practice of attending celebrations important to his friends. That he did not do so for Father Dave attests to the amount of activity needing his attention in Alaska.

Most on his mind were the many missions that had yet to be visited, and his concern for the Natives' lack of preparation for the government intervention. Father Fox had reported on the government's efforts to integrate the Natives into city work and lifestyle and the consequent erosion of family life in the villages. The men of the village were given jobs in towns and were no longer supplying food for the family or preparing for the hunting season. Women were left to provide for the family and, most often, they received no salary compensation from their husbands. With this topic on his mind, the bishop began serious thinking about the need for Native Adult Education.

Immaculate Conception School Is Built

At the end of August, the bishop returned to Fairbanks and discovered that Father Anable's solution for a grade school building led him to purchase from the city six barracks and a supervisor's shack used by construction crews when they built the airport. Men were hard at work converting the seven buildings into one and constructing eight classrooms and a principal's office. The children and parents were ready to occupy the building. There remained a single major difficulty. There were no teachers. Presented with the problem the bishop shook his people to their conservative core by suggesting that they hire lay teachers. This suggestion coming at a time when religious teachers were usually readily available was well in advance of the times.

There was no expansion of its faculty when Immaculate Conception School opened on September 9 and 10 with Mass, ceremonies of blessing and celebration. Unfortunately unless more teachers could be found, no more grades could be added. This problem Bishop Gleeson left to the school's administration while he journeyed to Juneau and Sitka, and from there to "the outside."

He returned home and repacked his bags for a flight to Anchorage with Father Gallant on September 30. There they joined with the people in their large and joyous celebrations for Reverend Robert D. O'Flanagan, their longtime pastor. Father O'Flanagan, as Bishop of the Diocese of Juneau would reside in the Capitol City making some of the celebrations in Anchorage a form of farewell.

On October 3, 1951 Archbishop Thomas A. Connelly of Seattle, to whose authority Juneau would be subject, ordained Father O'Flanagan as Bishop in Anchorage. There was little time to rest before Bishops Gleeson, O'Flanagan and six other clergymen flew from Anchorage to Juneau. They arrived in good time to practice in the Church of the Nativity of the Blessed Virgin Mary for the installation the next morning.

Memories of his own installation just three years earlier came to Gleeson's mind as he delivered the homily that morning. As before, celebration for the town took place in the evening. This time the gathering welcomed a new bishop into a new diocese, and they also reminisced with the bishop they had come to know and respect but were now losing.

Bishop Gleeson's Vicariate of Northern Alaska had lost its largest city. The Church in Alaska had gained its first Diocese. During the morning of October 8, Gleeson wished the new bishop well and left for Fairbanks without Father Conwell who remained in Junea to assist Bishop O'Flanagan until Christmas.

From Juneau Bishop Gleeson hurried to his mission parish where, except for a couple of quick trips to the city, he devoted the remainder of October and early November to business in Nenana.

On the eighth of November he boarded a plane for Seattle where he changed planes to fly to Washington, D.C. and the

United States Bishops' annual conference. Coincidentally, Gleeson's return from the meetings brought him into Fairbanks at the same time as Brother Aloysius B. Laird, S.J., who was on his way to Nenana to help with the work at St. Theresa's. On December 6 they traveled to Nenana and worked for the remainder of December on Advent and Christmas activities and the manual labor necessary to finish the Church/residence building.

Building and Fire: 1952

Brother and bishop fell victim to the flu on January 2; nonetheless, the latter made his usual Fairbanks visit on the weekend. Shortly, thereafter he began his visits to the coastal missions where the severe weather forced a delay of the annual consultors' meeting. A letter from Father O'Connor places him in Hooper Bay during the second week of March. Father says, Bishop Gleeson spent three days with me and then departed by dog team to Chevak. I worried as a storm came up almost before the team was out of sight.

The harsh weather conditions may account for Father Fox having time to write a lengthy letter to the Jesuit Father General at this time. Some of that missive gives an indication of the speed with which Native life and customs were changing. A quotation from the letter follows:

Both the religious as well as the economic life of my people may change soon as the result of a new government policy. Our government seems convinced that the Native economy could be improved by inducing the more skilled Natives to move to larger cities. There, it believes, these Eskimos would find opportunity to use their skill, and thus earn more money to raise their standard of living.

In accordance with this conviction, jobs in various places were offered last spring. Besides those who went to the various canneries during the fishing season, quite a group from two of my stations went to work near the city of Anchorage. From there some of them were taken to various other government jobs.

Planes started to pick up the men the latter part of April. They had agreed to stay on the job for six months. They were to buy their food and clothing from the local traders. The hiring agents assured both the men as well as the traders that the wages, amounting to about $3000.00 per man, were to be sent home regularly to the families left behind, or the trader who was advancing the things needed by the family. In theory, the plan looked very good... the writer...did not like it...nor did most of the families that were left without their head.

The glowing reports soon stopped coming. Nor did much money come. Large groups from some of the other villages returned home as soon as they had earned enough to pay their way over and back home. (Paying their travel expenses was the penalty for not sticking to their contract...) The families went deeper and deeper into debt; the women did injurious hard work. And for services in church we had practically only women and children all summer...when finally all the men came back...they had little more than to cover their debt at the store.... They had lost their summer fishing and hunting, had no wood ready for the winter...and were not prepared for the mink-hunting season.... They had nothing left (of their salaries).

The letter goes on then to describe the procurement of an electric light plant with financial help from the bishop. *The free light and power,* Father says, *will be a factor contributing to village regularity in retiring and rising. It starts at 6:30 A.M., and stops at 10:00 P.M. The trouble and expense involved in furnishing one's own light will be a deterrent from keeping late hours, as well as from many consequent evils.*

Father also makes note in his report, that the new village of St. Marys is growing, and that he as the mission Superior is in full charge of both mission and village.

Meanwhile in the Interior

The coastal weather did not reach Tok during March while the bishop was away, and the La Bree family took Father Buchanan to the store. They fitted him with *boots with leather tops and rubber bottoms.* They said, *You have to wear them. Sweating, itchy feet in the summer...sweating, freezing feet when its cold, but you have to wear them...*

The bishop did finally returned to Fairbanks on April 4 when he came from Bethel. Immediately Sisters Maurice and Judith, from Immaculate Conception school obtained an appointment to discuss the question of teachers for ICS. Again he suggested that they hire lay teachers. This time they took him at his word and left determined to find lay teachers.

The next day the bishop was on his way back to Nenana where he stayed until after Easter. Between sawing and sanding at St. Theresa's site, he set up a date with Father Buchanan to travel to Tok via Anchorage. The purpose of the trip was to inspect the chapels Father had built and to make a final decision about the location of the Glennallen chapel.

Inspecting the chapels is a suspect excuse because Bishop Gleeson had fussed when Father Fallert took him by dogsled to see his new chapel. Of course, Father Buchanan was a much younger pastor and seeing his chapels may well have been a matter of real inspection.

Their itinerary is not a matter of record, but if they did indeed go by way of Anchorage, they either took a plane or a train south and then picked up a car in Anchorage. Taking the Glenn Highway they would have passed farms being cultivated by pioneers who accepted the United States government's offer of free land in the Matanuska Valley for anyone willing to work it. This river valley through the Talkeetna Mountains provides beautiful scenery. Finally arriving at Glennallen, as the crow flies, something over 350 miles, they looked at some possible locations for the future Glennnallen chapel before continuing on the Tok Cut Off through the foothills of the Wrangell Mountains to inspect the new chapels at Tok Junction and Northway. These were completed and insured by December 1, 1951. Father Buchanan liked to say, *finished and insured on $30.00 and a Chevrolet.*

A letter from Father Buchanan dated August 5, 1952 gives some insight into his successful building projects *on $30.00.* A paragraph of the letter says: *I was having a thoughtful cup of coffee at the Buffalo Lodge when Mr. Stirwalt of Delta walked in, sat on the stool beside me and said, "...I understand you're looking for some land to build your chapel...I've got just the lot. Want to see it?"*

It was beautiful...right at the junction of the Richardson Highway and Alcan....One of his choicest lots and the most perfect spot for the new chapel. "It's yours, he said."

Father Buchanan returned the bishop to Fairbanks in June. It was then that Father Anable received permission to build the barge he proposed for Andreafski. Before settling for a stay in Nenana, the bishop made a quick visit to Tanana.

Two months later Father Boileau, assistant pastor of Immaculate Conception Church, took a FBI course in Washington, D.C. He had barely caught his breath when he returned home before he received word of his appointment as pastor of the parish with installation delayed until further word from the bishop.

The Little Sisters of Jesus Arrive in Alaska

According to Father Louis L. Renner, the installation was delayed until Bishop Gleeson returned from Nome where he was welcoming three Little Sisters of Jesus on August 25. He was particularly pleased to have these Sisters because they were not interested in, or even allowed, to work in the time honored places of school or hospital that most religious occupied. Their calling was for positions in the blue-collar workplace.

The bishop relished this presence among the workers as a means of raising religious awareness and love of God. Eventually, some of the Little Sisters, as they were affectionately called, lived and worked among the people on Little Diomede Island, and, for many years, a group lived and worked in Fairbanks. After welcoming the Sisters, Bishop Gleeson finished his visitations in the coastal villages and returned to Fairbanks in late August to set the date for the installation of Father Boileau, his friend since Sheridan days.

At the novitiate in Sheridan, George Boileau had volunteered to cook during the summer. Now Father Boileau was stepping into more than a pro tem cooking stint. The new pastor would be inheriting the headache of paying for the newly built grade school as well as that of resolving the question posed by the graduating eighth grade children. Where would the children go to school in September 1952?

Father George T. Boileau Pastor

Installed as pastor of I.C. during the morning of September 14, Father Boileau's celebration came fully alive in the evening when the bishop, along with Fathers Anable, Cunningham, Conwell, and Sullivan, Reynolds, Pettid and Brother Fidelis, from Ladd AFB, arrived. Early the next morning, the men from Ladd and the bishop left. The latter promised to return the next weekend to help on Sunday. This he did for the next several weekends when he often said two Masses in Fairbanks and another in Nenana.

A letter from Father David McAstocker of Bellarmine days, written on September 22, 1952 reached the bishop on one of his weekend visits. The letter, an acknowledgment of the bishop's anniversary telegram in 1951 points out an important characteristic of Francis Gleeson. Father Dave says:

It was very thoughtful of you to remember me by that gracious telegram on the occasion of my golden jubilee. Your kindness will never be forgotten.

When I entered the Order my whole ambition was to go to Alaska, and instead I went to a sanatorium and a few off-places. At one of the off-places I met a wonderful man who had the most even temper I have ever witnessed in another man. The man was Father Francis Gleeson.

Invitations to R and R

At the invitation of Father Conwell, the bishop spent the first two days of October visiting in Fairbanks with Father Paul O'Connor on the government's Commission for Housing, Brother Carl F. Wickart chief maintenance man at Immaculate Conception parish for many years, and Fathers Buchanan, Cunningham, and Boileau. It was a comfortable and relaxing time for all these good friends and concluded with a tour of Fairbanks by Bishop Gleeson and Fathers Conwell and Boileau. Their objective was to find property suitable for a church and rectory on the south side of town to take the burden off the existing inadequate building before considering any further school structures.

During these early days in October the bishop had another bout of flu; however, he continued to commute into Fairbanks every weekend to assist with parish services. This prompted Father Conwell to host another few days of rest and relaxation. On the twenty-second the bishop returned to Nenana to meet with Father Henry G. Hargreaves from Bethel.

Fathers Conwell and Boileau continued their quest for property near Weeks Field; that is, the city airport. His shopping instincts aroused, Father Conwell found land for a possible future high school as well as several other sites for consideration. The following letter from Father Buchanan speaks of one of the tasks that the Chancellor of the Diocese undertook.

Carl Peterson a mechanic in Fairbanks picked up Father Conwell and we (Conwell and Buchanan) met in Tok. Dusk saw us in the Copper Valley. Past barking dogs and curious Indian children until we stood on the banks of the Tazlina River. There we studied out the prospects for a Mission School. The land was clean and level...the river poured by...the fishing was good...farming was possible with a minimum danger of floods...there was good timber and as far as the eye could see, magnificent scenery. Father Conwell is going to take care of acquiring the land.

Then, on October 27, Father Buchanan and the bishop traveled down the highway bound for Seattle. Father Buchanan would seek materials for his building projects, and the bishop would board a plane for Washington, D. C. and the annual Bishops' Conference. While at the Conference, it is safe to say that there were a number of conversations about the United States Senate action that once again quashed hopes for Alaska statehood.

Bishops from the northwest undoubtedly discussed with Bishop Gleeson the truth or lack of it concerning the impact of fishing rights in the Territory. In his book <u>Alaska, A Bicentennial History</u>, William R. Hunt says that Winton C. Arnold, director of The Trade Association of the Salmon Industry in 1951, listed the difficulties that would befall Alaska if it was admitted to the Union. Chief among the troubles would be the support of state services. Of more importance to the Union would be the impairment of international treaties and the transfer of federal lands to the state. He also referred to the aboriginal land claims that would become wholly confused. The bishop could speak knowledgeably about a number of these issues because of Fathers Endal and Convert's work.

Senator W. Magnuson of Washington favored statehood, but Senator Hugh Butler of Nebraska did not and very forcefully reiterated Winton Arnold's reasons for rejecting the bill before Congress. Along with Butler's arguments army interests lobbied government officials to consider moving the Boeing aircraft industry from Seattle to Wichita, Kansas as a precaution against Russian air attacks.

Ernest Gruening of Alaska put forth a counter suggestion that resulted in the stationing of more interceptor planes in Alaska and the building of the Distant Early Warning System (DEW Line) on the western and northern coasts of the Alaskan Peninsula. Clear, Alaska, named headquarters for the system, was a mission of the Nenana Church and thus well known to Bishop Gleeson.

When he returned from Washington, D.C. on December 6, the bishop had with him Father Lonneux. Father had been in a hospital in Seattle until Bishop Gleeson brought him to the hospital in Fairbanks where he could be near those with whom he had worked. The missionaries could be agitated about their bishop's spending for building and its belt tightening effects, but they had to admire his compassion.

Back to work at home Gleeson officiated at Fort Greely on December 13 for a Holy Name Society Communion Mass and breakfast in the morning, and a Confirmation ceremony in the afternoon. The next day he returned to Fairbanks and left for Nenana on the seventeenth.

A Disastrous Fire

Advent of 1952 was to be the first community preparation for Christmas celebrations in the newly renovated Nenana church. Anticipation was high among the people of St. Theresa's parish, indeed everywhere in the village, for the renewal of community until December 19. That morning as Gleeson was beginning the Sacrifice of the Mass he heard a strange crackling noise in his living quarters. Leaving the altar to investigate, he found the wall behind the kitchen stove completely enveloped in flames. He hurriedly stripped off his vestments and ran to ask a neighbor to give the alarm.

In a letter to the missionaries, Father Conwell describes the scene:

The fire was very spectacular in the early morning. Fortunately, there was no wind, so the flames went straight up. The temperature was about five below zero. For a time it was feared that the fire would spread to the next door neighbor's house only ten feet from the church, so all furnishings were removed from it. If the church walls had fallen, this house would probably have caught fire, but the sturdily built walls remained standing...

Although firemen responded immediately, the flames destroyed the interior of the building and all its contents— personal belongings, books, papers, vestments and sacred vessels, gold pectoral cross— before the men could repair their defective equipment. Only the basement remained within the standing walls when the fire was extinguished.

The bishop regretted the destruction of his books, but mourned the loss of his pectoral crosses, one of which had belonged to the martyred Archbishop Charles J. Seghers and the other to Archbishop William H. Gross, C.Ss.R., of Oregon City. Both had been passed down through Bishop Crimont, and were significant historical relics.

Father Conwell's letter goes on to say that the cause of the fire is uncertain, but it is thought that possibly a spark ignited the soot in the stove pipe, or perhaps there was a small explosion of coal gas in the kitchen range.

An Unexpected Result of the Fire

While waiting for spring weather and the opportunity to rebuild, the bishop is grateful to Jack Coghill for his offer to use the lobby in his new lodge for church services. There is less than a week before Christmas and the people of St. Theresa's fine plans for Christmas and New Year celebrations lay in ruins. The bishop's plans, too, lay in ashes. Father Conwell said, *The bishop was without a place to go for Christmas. Our needs were sufficiently provided for here in Fairbanks. (The Army chaplains are sorry they didn't hear about that—they would have asked him to go to McKinley Park, which didn't have a priest for Christmas. Many on the hotel staff are Catholics, and a number of servicemen were there for the holidays.) I had been at Point Barrow two weeks before, to take care of the spiritual needs of Catholic personnel at the Navy petroleum project. The commanding officer, a Catholic asked me whether there were any possibilities of having a priest for Christmas. I had told him there were none....*At the last minute, Father Conwell remembered the commander at the Barrow naval compound had asked for a priest for Christmas; he quickly suggested that Bishop Gleeson contact him.

It was a fortuitous contact. The bishop's Mass at the naval installation, was in American history the first Christmas midnight Mass ever celebrated by a bishop at this northernmost settlement. He stayed five days, visited the villagers, and the Alaska Native Service's school and hospital, toured the navy camp and some historical landmarks, and went by "weasel" to Point Barrow, the northernmost point of Alaska.

The experience heightened his interest in establishing a Catholic mission at Barrow.

Photo by JY Studio, Fairbanks

Photo by Lens Unlimited, Fairbanks

Fr. Fox Fr. Anable Fr. Paul O'Conner Fr. Renner
Mt. Village Procurator Housing Com. U. of. Ak.

COLLEGE PREP SCHOOL FOR ALASKANS
COPPER VALLEY SCHOOL
Glennallen, Alaska
Jesuits-Sisters of St. Ann-Lay Volunteers

The former St. Mary's mission and boarding school complex on the Andreafsky River near where it flows into the lower Yukon. Today it serves as the center for the Native Ministry Training Program. Eskimo deacon retreats and various workshops generally take place here. (Photo by Robert K. Betz)

Chaneliak

Nenana

Holy Cross Church Convent School

Building and Rebuilding: 1953

Bishop Gleesen went to Nenana with an insurance adjuster on January 2 and Fathers Conwell and Boileau attended a City Planning and Zoning Committee meeting to ask for permission to build a church on the Pan American property near Weeks Field. The permission was readily granted. The insurance adjuster was not quite so ready to bring smiles to the bishop's face. He did determine that the coverage was enough to rebuild on a smaller scale.

In this part of a letter by Father Conwell to the missionaries he explains the financial issues of the Nenana fire:

In a way, the fire is a blessing in disguise. The building, built thirty years ago by Father Francis M. Monroe, S.J., when Nenana was a "city" of two to three thousand people, was too large for present needs, was hard to heat, and was awkwardly arranged. The front half of the building was the church, the rear half was divided into two stories of living quarters. If the Bishop rebuilds on the same floor and foundations, he will probably have the church occupy the same space as before, but with a much lower ceiling, and have one-story living quarters in the rear.

On the thirteenth of January the bishop and Father Conwell inspected the land near Weeks Field as a prospective site for a new church and residence. They made no decision, but Bishop Gleeson thought the piece looked a little smaller than they were told. When they had finished shopping the bishop went home to Father Hargreaves, his visitor from Bethel. During the visit Father was admitted to St. Joseph hospital. There is nothing to say what he suffered from, but the flu was prevalent at the time, and, off and on, the bishop was ill with it. As Father Hargreaves recovered, Father Lonneux, in the same hospital, died on January 21.

Father had spent twenty-eight years in Northern Alaska with the Eskimos. He composed, in the Eskimo language, booklets on the Mass, a variety of prayers, a hymnal and a translation of the <u>Baltimore</u> <u>Catechism</u>. A memorial in <u>Jesuits</u> <u>in</u> <u>Alaska,</u> credits Father Lonneux with many things. Besides being a first class missionary, he was a carpenter, a cook, an actor, a mimic, a benevolent Dictator and a thorough monopolizer of every conversation.

Many of the Jesuits in Alaska assembled in Fairbanks for his funeral on January 24. The Requiem Mass was celebrated at the Church of the Immaculate Conception with Father Boileau as celebrant because the bishop had succumbed to the flu on the twenty-second and had been admitted to the hospital. After the Mass the burial had to be postponed because workmen could not be found to open the grave.

Later that day the bishop, released from the hospital, prepared to take a plane for Kotzebue on the twenty-fifth. He would then fly to Nome and eventually to Andreafski. Many of those present for the funeral continued on to St. Mary's where they assembled with the bishop on February 10 for the annual mission conference. It was the largest and most diversified gathering of Jesuits to date.

They discussed the impact of Francis M. Menager's illness and Father Lonneux's death on the work of the missions in northern Alaska. Both Menager and Lonneux had been real longtime assets to mission endeavors. As a result of that discussion, some opposed a new mission at Barrow considering the expansion impractical because of the shrinking number of priests. Still others approved a priestly presence at Barrow if only at intervals. It was finally agreed that Father Tom Cunningham should minister to Barrow.

St. Mary's Mission School evoked more lively discussion that finished with an enthusiastic vote of approval to the proposal that the school offer a solid academic program, K through 12. The program was to be designed to launch the boarders into higher education or an informed place in village adult life.

The men then considered the grave structural and economic problems at Holy Cross. They deliberated about the recently purchased laundry equipment, and the big new dynamo to generate power for the equipment that was being purchased through the generosity of Most Reverend John Wright, Bishop of Worcester, Massachusetts and Monsignors J. Boutin, W. Ducharme and Father O. Cheverette. Aware of all the improvements and the educational status, the consultors and missionaries found the continuing financial problems a huge stumbling block. No decisions were made on that issue.

Another question of great concern had to do with the unions and the fishing and canning industry that brought so many Catholic Eskimos away from their homes each year. As previously recorded, Fathers Endal and Convert were deeply involved with that situation, and 1953 found Father Clifford Carroll, S.J., investigating the union activity.

Finally, the gathering debated the advantage versus disadvantage of various forms for recording parish information. They settled on standardized parochial record cards for Baptism, Confirmation, Marriage, and Death. When old records were copied on to the new forms, the Vicariate would be in conformity with Canon 470.

Weathered in after the business meetings, those who had not seen each other for several years were happy for the extended visit; yet, by the end of the week most everyone, including the bishop, departed. Later, from Bethel, Bishop Gleeson wrote Father Conwell, *It took nineteen days to get on to Nelson Island and sixteen to get off, but I made it.* Probably on one of those snow bound days with no outside communication, Stalin died in Moscow on March 5 without anyone on the coast from Bethel to Nome being aware of the world headlines.

Finally Bishop Gleeson made it back home from the stormy coast and reclaimed his rooms at Immaculate Conception on March 24. More or less marooned in Fairbanks while the Nenana building was being restored the bishop continued with the process of looking for land on which to build a new church on the south side of the city. That was an audacious activity while Jesuit missioners were chaffing under the economic impact of St. Mary's construction. Society members, already greatly distressed over the prohibition on bargain buying, did not take kindly to any report concerning further building. Nevertheless, giving no indication that he recognized their dismay with his building programs, the bishop in April of 1953 quietly authorized the purchase of a small parcel of land from Pan American Airlines.

On April 4 he officiated and preached at the ten and twelve o'clock Masses at Ladd Field, and attended the public reception

Chaplain Edward J. Pettid, S.J., arranged to allow personnel to meet and visit with the bishop. Four days later, Gleeson flew to Oregon where he stayed at Sheridan while he assembled replacements for altar linens, candle sticks, and similar church appointments that were lost in the Nenana fire. According to his correspondence with Father Conwell, checks and personal mail destroyed in that fire continued to cause confusion.

That trip to Oregon was also an opportunity for the bishop to celebrate with old friends on April 26, Bellarmine High School's Silver Jubilee. Former students, faculty and staff recalled evenings of repartee, the fundraiser saved from disaster by plentiful wine, sparse dinners with candy bars for a late snack, rock-strewn playing fields, the daily care of farm animals and like topics. These events that almost seemed like matters of life and death twenty-five years before were recalled with proper nostalgia.

His energy restored, Bishop Gleeson returned to Nenana to hire a carpenter. From May 5 to 10 the carpenter cleared away the debris left by the fire to expose a floor in good condition. The carpenter would raise a new building on the old foundation and flooring while the bishop divided his time between Nenana and Fairbanks. Fairbanks duties included a Confirmation ceremony at Ladd Airforce Base on the seventeenth and graduation ceremonies for seventeen graduates of Immaculate

Conception grade school during the month of May. Of the seventeen grade school graduates, five were boys. This was the fourth graduation from the grade school, and the largest to date.

On the eighteenth a purchase deal for about an acre and a half of land bounded by Vagabond Smith and Calum Streets was closed for $10,000. A week later word came that Mr. Robert F. Corrigal, S.J., had arrived in Nulato to help Father Baud build a new house. Because it was one of the first mission houses put up when priests came to the Alaska Natives, it desperately needed repairs even when the bishop first saw it five years before.

Everyone—bishop, priests and Brother—attached to Immaculate Conception was tired from the busy month of May, and all were happy to accept an invitation to dinner on June 8 at the Kirsch family cabin on Harding Lake. It was a thirty-six mile scenic ride down the Richardson Highway and provided the group with a wonderful afternoon of relaxation away from routine business.

For the next two weeks of June, the bishop traveled back and forth from his parish to his office several times a week until, on the twenty-third, he rented a cabin across from the rapidly rising church. Thereafter he reigned from his cabin as building overseer and Vicar Apostolic with his office in Fairbanks.

Dreams of a School in the Tok Region

Buchanan finished his fourth chapel while the bishop toiled in Nenana. This last chapel at Glennallen was situated on Glenn road more to the west than the other three chapels, and its completion was a signal to Father Buchanan to present the bishop with his plans for a school in the Tok area. John Buchanan, a man built like a fullback in the prime of life, full of energy, enthusiasm, and profound faith in God, was a Scholastic when he taught at Holy Cross. While there he became convinced that Native children would profit greatly from higher education and intimate acquaintance with other cultures.

He envisioned his new school on the Tazlina River with an enrollment of mixed ethnic groups and a curriculum designed to prepare all, but especially Alaska Native children, as leaders among their peers. He was prepared, too, to raise building and transportation costs through donations. "Paid costs" were the magic words that often obtained the bishop's permission to build.

This time was no exception. With permission obtained, Father Buchanan drove to Fairbanks to pick up the Vicariate

Chancellor and take him to the location proposed for the school. As they rode south on the Richardson Highway, Father Buchanan seemed to forget that Father Conwell had seen this area the year before. Filled with enthusiasm Buchanan waxed eloquent on the advantages and beauty of the site. The land, he eulogized as clear and level, the river poured by, the fishing was good, farming was possible, there was good timber as far as the eye could see and magnificent scenery. On arrival Father Conwell, agreed with the vision presented. He also noted the advantageous location between Valdez, Anchorage and Fairbanks. In fact, the only drawback from the priest's viewpoint was a lack of sweet water. If Bishop Gleeson had heard the conversation, he would have had flashbacks to Sheridan in the nineteen forties.

Through Territorial Delegate Bob Bartlett, Father Conwell sent a claim description to Congress with a request for sixty acres, and obtained the grant with no problem. On June 26 Father Buchanan reported that good progress was being made on obtaining materials for the new school and delivery of them was promised in time for construction to begin the next year. As he examined plans for a boarding school complex, he hoped it would one day include a university.

On the Fairbanks front during July the bishop went to Nome to Confirm a summer vacation school class prepared by two

Sisters from Fairbanks. He continued his visitations by flying to McGrath, Holy Cross, and St. Mary's. At the last stop he inspected Father Anable's canning barge being constructed on the river and asked about the fish camps that Father was supervising. With his visitation completed, the bishop returned to his office in Fairbanks before traveling to Nenana on the eighth. Four days later Father James W. Plamondon, S.J., joined the bishop in Fairbanks and accompanied him back to Nenana to install electrical wiring in the new church. The next day Fathers Boileau, Wilcock and Gaffney arrived by small plane for a one-day visit to see the new building. That afternoon Boileau and Gaffney returned to Fairbanks by plane, and Father Wilcock took the scenic railroad route in the evening.

Flying to Juneau the next week, Father Wilcock inquired about the feasibility of acquiring Russian Uniate priests for Dillingham, Alaska. The answer, as Bishop Gleeson anticipated, was a suggestion that Alaskan priests learn to use Eastern Rite liturgies and prayers.

To cap the month of August, the bishop tripped over a log in St. Theresa's parking area and fell. He was only slightly injured, but it was enough to tie him to his desk for a bit. There he scrutinized papers being readied for the diocesan divisions he foresaw for the Church in Alaska. Readying the documents he traced the dramatic expansion of Vicariate ownership of land and buildings to Father Buchanan's activities on the eastern border and his own divesting of Society of Jesus Alaskan possessions.

Over several months, Father Conwell, writing for Bishop Gleeson, contacted Fathers Small, Schultheis, and Paul P. Sauer regarding the transfer of ownership, of Jesuit holdings in Alaska. On September 22, 1953, the Society signed the necessary papers transferring its properties under the title of the Pioneer Educational Society to the Catholic Bishop of Northern Alaska, a religious corporation sole organized and existing according to the laws of the Territory of Alaska. The transfer represented a large Society investment and disconcerted some Jesuits; however, it also represented a major step toward freeing the Vicariate from financial entanglements with the Society and cleared the way for future diocesan status.

Father Edmund Anable also traced the transfer of property and, as procurator, worried more than usual about the money trail. It prompted him to write Father Provincial a letter in which he gave chapter and verse concerning Bishop Gleeson's dangerous spending. He declared the Vicariate to be bankrupt—more than $30,000 in debt.

The property transfer also disturbed the men of the Society of Jesus on the Alaskan missions and the political doings in the Territory aggravated that uneasiness. With the question of statehood uppermost in their minds the priests were monitoring, as well as they were able, the activities of the group of senators holding hearings on the question.

These senators interviewed about a hundred forty people, none of them Jesuits, and then returned to the states where Senator Hugh Butler, speaking to his Nebraska constituents, reported that most of the clamor for statehood came from politicians who wanted to run for office. Democratic senators who participated in the hearings disagreed vigorously, but the opposition managed to delay congressional progress for another two years.

The fact that President Eisenhower favored statehood for Hawaii but opposed it for Alaska because the military could function better if Alaska remained a Territory may have helped silence Congress. Of course, Eisenhower's reasoning included the protection of a Republican majority in the Senate. The general feeling appeared to be that Alaska would be a Democratic state.

These hearings gave Bishop Gleeson and his builders in Nenana a topic for conversation during October until he boarded the train for Anchorage on the twenty-first on his way to visit Naknek, Dillingham, and Clarks Point. At the last stop he confirmed thirty-five. On the twenty-fourth he rested returning to Nenana by train. The following day, Father Lawrence Nevue and ten men came from Fairbanks to work on the interior finishing of the new St. Theresa's building.

With the bishop in Nenana, Father Boileau forbore to invite him when calling together twenty parishioners at Immaculate Conception on November 5 to discuss with them parish progress in general and the crowded condition of the church and school in particular. The meeting was intended to formulate some sound and adequate plans for future growth of the parish.

The committee agreed to meet regularly each Wednesday until they had resolved the needs to a workable and understandable basis. One of the problems addressed ideas for a new high school to accommodate graduates of Immaculate Conception grade school. A second problem pinpointed the impossibility of accepting all the applicants for the grade school, and a third looked at the growth of the city population with no way to accommodate a larger congregation in the church building.

Theoretically, parish planning did not concern the bishop; in reality, he had to give his permission to build and to apply for a loan. When he was consulted, he told the parishioners that he could not guarantee a loan because his credit had reached its limit. Unhappy, they returned to their worktable and looked to the pastor for possible solutions. Father Boileau responded by reminding the board that pledging funds for the needed school would be a way to celebrate the commemoration of the Marian Year and the Golden Jubilee of the founding of Immaculate Conception parish. Grumbling a bit about another fundraiser they nevertheless recognized this as a possible answer and began planning ways and means.

While these meetings were going on Father William H. Babb came as the new assistant pastor at Immaculate Conception. His appearance freed the bishop to move permanently to Nenana, and, more immediately, to prepare for the annual Bishops' Conference in the District of Columbia. While making his preparations to leave, Gleeson noted with satisfaction that the Nenana building was under roof and at the point of having bathroom tile installed, and that Father Spils was close to completing St. Mary's interior work.

His satisfaction grew when he returned from the east coast, to find that most of his furniture, files and clothing were in Nenana courtesy of Fathers Conwell and Babb who had carried his possessions over the new Tok road in a station wagon. Traveling the new road the priests made the trip in three and a half-hours. They reported the road to be fairly good except for some bumpy and rough patches. Its many curves and narrow width contributed to slow traffic.

A Golden Jubilee Year: 1954

The New Year began with a significant loss for the missions when Father Edward J. Pettid, S.J., Catholic Chaplain at Ladd Field, left that post on January 3. Father had worked well with the priests in Fairbanks and with the missionaries. However, everyone recognized that military personnel were routinely rotated and business went on until the new person was assimilated.

For the Catholic people of Fairbanks the parish building board was of major importance. The board met with the bishop on the sixth of January to present their plans for building a new grade school and converting the present one into a high school. In general he agreed with the program they proposed, and reminded them of the large down payment that preceded any actual work. The meeting adjourned with Father Boileau promising to try for a loan in Seattle.

At their February 17 meeting Father advised the board that neither state nor national agencies could make loans in Alaska and that the usual interest is five percent. His report was sweetened a little with assurances from the Jesuit Father Provincial and the Mother Provincial of the Providence Sisters that teachers would be available if a high school were started. The board concluded their deliberations with an affirmative vote for a drive to raise a hundred or a hundred and fifty thousand dollars and then try to borrow an additional hundred thousand from the local banks.

The next day, at a meeting of the Catholic School Association, Father Boileau announced that the school bus could be repaired only at considerable expense. The parish could no longer assume the burden of running the bus.

School bussing had been a question raised by the Territory while the bishop was residing in Juneau. There was no law against a government bus moving Catholic school children; however, the decision came down in Juneau to refuse private school bussing. The Association voted for a committee to be appointed and empowered to make the best possible arrangements for transportation.

While Father Boileau and his parishioners confronted school problems, the bishop hosted Father Rene Voillaune, Prior of the Little Brothers of Jesus, Sister Magdelene, Foundress of the Little Sisters of Jesus, Sister Jean, their Mother General, and Sister Jacqueline, Supervisor in America. The group arrived by Alaska Airlines from Seattle on Thursday, March 4, in the first week of Lent. This stop was part of a year long round the world tour of all their missions, and their conference with Bishop Gleeson had to do with possible work for their Sisters in Nome and other places in the Territory of Alaska.

From the conference with Bishop Gleeson the visitors went on to Nome to see the Little Sisters working there, and on March 17 Father Tom Cunningham, Father Voillaune and the Little Sisters traveled on the same plane to Bettles. The visitors seemed enthusiastic about the possibilities of getting established in Bettles where the Sisters would be near the nomadic Eskimos. The group returned that evening on the same Wien plane that took them to Bettles.

For his part, the bishop, after speaking with the travelers, drained the water pipes and closed the house in Nenana in preparation for a visitation tour of his own. From Fairbanks he and Father Conwell went to the Copper River on March 10 to visit the project in progress there only to discover that supplies were short due to travel difficulties during the winter months. Disappointed, they returned to Fairbanks after Mass the next day.

Four days later, March 16, the Immaculate Conception parish board organized teams to raise money for a new school. Father Boileau explained the plans at Masses on the twenty-first and brochures were distributed. On this date the bishop blessed their efforts with the following message:

It gives me great satisfaction to learn that the members of our Fairbanks parish are entering with enthusiasm into the plans of their Pastor to enlarge and improve local facilities to provide a more complete Catholic education for our young people.

The result will be a distinct service to God and country, a priceless benefit to our Catholic youth for many generations.

Team captains met in planning sessions each evening that week and Father Boileau with several members of the finance committee met at Ladd Field with Major Colnin, Captain of the military team, and the Army and Air Force Chaplains at Eielson and Ladd. Father was surprised and disappointed at the cool reception afforded by the chaplains who looked upon their parishes as separate entities from Fairbanks at the same time ignoring the many years military children had been educated at the expense of the Fairbanks parish. Finally, agreement was reached whereby the plan would be explained at Masses and a quiet drive among base personnel conducted.

While the people of Immaculate Conception worked at raising money for their parish, the bishop boarded Alaska Air for a Confirmation trip to Stebbins, St. Michael, Chaneliak, Alukanuk, Scammon Bay, Chevak and Bethel on the Bering Coast. He went also to Hooper Bay and Holy Cross. It was from St. Mary's that the bishop wrote to Father Conwell,

The new building makes living much more convenient and the gym and the chapel are real gems. There are only a few odds and ends to finish up. Good weather held for the whole three-week trip to ten widely spaced villages, and the train dropped him at Nenana on April 12, just in time for Holy Week.

His Nenana people and those of the surrounding villages were happy to have their pastor for Easter Sunday even though he flew to Fairbanks in the afternoon. In Fairbanks, although he was scheduled to attend a public reception for visiting military clergy, he heard, from excited board members and an elated Father Boileau, about the large crowds at all the Masses and the $134,057 reached in the school drive. The news made for happy conversation as Fathers Boileau and Conwell accompanied the bishop to Ladd Field for the reception.

Honored were Bishop William R. Arnold, Military Delegate of the Military Ordinariate; and Brigadier General Father Terence P. Finnegan, Deputy Chief of Chaplains of the Air Force who were visiting military bases in Alaska. The two priests and Bishop Gleeson were included in the dinner invitation extended to all the Chaplains by Mr. and Mrs. Alvin Johnson. The couple served the dinner at their home. On the Monday after Easter the bishop, the hospital Sisters and the clergy of Fairbanks attended a special showing at the Empress Theater of "The Robe." This was the first Cinemascope picture shown in Fairbanks.

The next day it was back to work for everyone. The bishop had the company of Father Nevue as far as Nenana. Father then continued on to the next station where he planned to begin visiting each of the railroad stops. At each station he would say Mass, administer the Sacraments, and survey the town from the point of view of Church needs. He estimated that this would take about two weeks. His findings would go into a report for the bishop.

In Nenana the bishop began orienting himself to duties awaiting him. One of the first duties was to write a letter to the new Provincial of the Oregon Province, Father Henry Joseph Schultheis, who would be taking office that day, April 20. Father Henry J. Schultheis, S.J., replaced Father Harold Small, long time friend of Bishop Gleeson. Small had been a new Provincial when Gleeson was appointed to Alaska. Now, more than five years later, Father Small would have some time to regain his energy when Father Schultheis took over. Sitting down at his desk Bishop Gleeson immediately wrote a letter congratulating Father Schultheis and assuring him of prayers and best wishes.

The Provincial had to determine the fate of Sheridan, the novitiate for which Gleeson had been Rector. It had, over the years, become a large school. Through diligent, thorough searching a sweet water supply had been found, but the building had only a temporary exterior finish. The question for Father Schultheis to answer: should the building's exterior be finished, or should the school be moved to another location. A thorny question!

After ten days of attending to problems and work at Nenana, the bishop flew, on May 2, to Nome and from there to Little Diomede Island. It was the first recorded visit of a bishop to the island. An historic event for the Catholic Church. While he was on the island, he administered the Sacrament of Confirmation to the thirty candidates who had been prepared by Father Tom the month before.

The island, just two miles from Soviet Diomede Island, has no landing facilities and its almost vertical, rocky sides whipped by waves of the Bering Strait make approach by water extremely dangerous. Eskimos and visitors make the journey to and from the island by skin boat. This bishop's arrival by plane made the visit especially memorable. Although Bishop Gleeson made no more visits to Little Diomede, he did give The Little Sisters of Jesus permission to reside there. Sisters from Africa had augmented the original small group.

By May 6 he was once more in Nenana and ten days later he arrived in Fairbanks by small plane. At two o'clock in the afternoon, he administered the Sacrament of Confirmation for thirty people at Immaculate Conception and at four o'clock repeated the ceremony for twenty-five others at the base chapel of Ladd Field. Then he was off again visiting mission stations throughout Alaska. At one point he took the time to write to Father Babb in Fairbanks the following directive:

Dear Fr. Babb:

Please deposit this very precious check in our account. It is several thousand larger this year than ever before and arrived on the Feast of the Sacred Heart. I have sent a check for this same amount to Fr. Anable so it won't help our account much but will likely raise up the drooping spirits of the Mission Procurator.

Historic Parish Celebrates Fifty Years

The Golden Jubilee festivities for the founding of the Immaculate Conception parish began with a Solemn Pontifical Mass. "Jessin's Weekly" for Thursday, July 8, 1954 gave good coverage for the founding event. Part of the main article says:

On July 1, 1904, Very Rev. Raphael Crimont, S.J. Prefect Apostolic of Alaska and Father Francis M. Monroe, S.J. came together for the first time to the two-year-old mining camp center which was to become Fairbanks. Following the discovery of gold by Felix Pedro, several thousand people rushed into the promising area and among them were many Catholics. The price of real estate and labor was beyond the means of the Jesuits, so a group of local men organized for the purpose of raising the necessary finances for a church. A rough 65 by 30-

214

foot structure was erected at the cost of $6,512. A keg of eight-penny nails cost $50 at that time.

Father Monroe traveled all over the mining camps and around in Interior Alaska soliciting help and finally raised $4,795.75. This, added to the $3,051.00 the committee of men had collected, enabled the missionary to pay off the debt and decorate the church and also install a small library along with his living quarters. Not a few people in the camp criticized Father severely for what they thought was too large a building, saying there never would be enough Catholics in Fairbanks to justify the size.

Now, fifty years later, people assembled for Mass on the grounds adjoining St. Joseph's Hospital and the church but were driven inside by rain. The deluge cleansed and sweetened the air outside while inside the church and parish hall where Mass was being celebrated a joyous atmosphere prevailed.

Following the Mass there was a breakfast for the resident clergy and their guests Father John Buchanan of Tok, Lawrence Haffie of Bethel, Leo Pesset, Air Force chaplain from Ladd, and Mr. Joe Obersinner from Alma College. Another repast followed in the late afternoon and then a dinner for the clergy at the Country Club. Dignitaries at the dinner included service chaplains from all over Alaska, Bishop O'Flanagan, Father Harold Small, S.J., and Bishop Alexis Monet, O.M.I., from

Whitehorse, Yukon. In the evening a large number of parishioners enjoyed themselves at the public reception in the parochial school hall. Most of the conversations, even among the dignitaries, were enlivened by a rumor about a proposed regional school in Copper Valley.

In Bishop Gleeson's tribute during the Jubilee he prayed:

The keynote of any jubilee, and especially one such as ours, is gratitude. Today then we turn our hearts in gratitude to God and to those noble men and women from the ranks of both the religious and the laity who have pioneered the work of the Church in Fairbanks. May the pioneer's courage and spirit of sacrifice ever be to us an incentive to emulate their efforts with untiring zeal.

When the celebrating was over, Bishop Gleeson took Bishop O'Flanagan by train to admire the northern Alaska wilderness and the new building in Nenana. The two returned to Fairbanks that evening for Bishop O'Flanagan to board his plane for Juneau and for Bishop Gleeson to resume his Confirmation tour on the next day. Gleeson went to Holy Cross and afterward to St. Mary's where he assisted at an unusual event.

Father Fox's annual Conference for the villages on the Yukon was in session. The Conference always drew a great number from each village, but this year three entire villages took to boats of all kinds to assemble at St. Mary's. From the upper Yukon, Marshall to Akulurak in the Delta, the Eskimos came. They were all anxious to witness the rites on August 15 for the clothing of the first three Novices of the Oblates of Our Lady of the Snows, a religious community of Eskimo women founded and nurtured by Father Fox. The work of the women was to be a catechetical contact with people the priests could not visit on a regular basis.

On his first visit to Mountain Village, Bishop Gleeson had asked the people if they would support a group of religious women. They had deliberated and assented. Over the years no established group of religious came, but this community did blossom from that seed. The Eskimos had reason to be proud.

The reception day for the new religious was probably the last time Brother Alfred and the bishop visited. Twelve days later on August 27 Brother Alfred Murphy, S.J., died. Brother had been with the St. Mary's community for thirty-eight of his forty-one years in Alaska. He had kept the Akulurak orphanage alive with the fish he and his crew of Natives brought in yearly, and the wood and freight and driftwood they gathered. Just weeks before, he brought the Akulurak pilgrims to the new school and helped them settle. Usually Bishop Gleeson tried to be present for the funeral services of his Jesuit brothers. This time he was on the Bering Seacoast and could not attend.

A kind of legend grew up around one of his visits to that region. The story circulated is something like this:

When the plane taking him to Chevak landed in Hooper Bay, the tide was out, so they rode at anchor at the edge of a mud flat some half-mile wide. Residents customarily plodded through the mud in hip boots, but the bishop had not come prepared for this, and the boots offered him by the Native men were much too small. Next, the men proposed to carry him in piggyback, but no one was able to transport his very considerable weight. At length they seized upon a kayak, took it to the plane and coaxed the bishop into it. They then guided it to shallow water where they hoisted it upon their shoulders and carried him to the village where they were met and escorted into the church by the whole congregation singing hymns in their Native language.

After Mass the next morning, Bishop Gleeson hurried out of the church to ask the men to repeat the kayak scene so he could take a picture to show the Pope. Needless to say, he had no picture to take to Rome the next month, but the request probably resulted in the legend.

AN AD LIMINA VISIT TO ROME

Did the bishop fudge a bit on the time he gave to the coastal visits? If so, it would be a most uncharacteristic act. His work at home was done as thoroughly as his preparations for the ad limina visit were done. He was ready to give a stewardship accounting of his first five years as Vicar Apostolic of Alaska and the itinerary for his trip reads like a marvelous vacation package.

This visit to Rome began on September 15 when Bishop Gleeson traveled from Nenana to Fairbanks. Five days later he boarded a plane for Seattle and on to Portland, Oregon. By the twenty-sixth he arrived in Montana where he said a Pontifical Mass at St. Ignatius for the Mission's Centennial celebration. From there he flew to New York where he joined Father Jules Convert. A short letter dated October 7 from Father Conwell probably reached the bishop in New York. It said,

Many thanks for your letter of Oct. 5. The Little Brother is Father Wsewolod de Rocheau, 23 rue Oudinet, Paris, France.

It's good to know that bankruptcy is no longer threatening. I'll pay back $5,000.00 to Father Boileau, and I'll tell him that Father Anable will send $10,000.00 more...

...Douglas Preston was elected mayor in the big election a couple of days ago...We had a few wisps of snow, and more snow is threatening...

While in New York, Father Convert and the bishop arranged to buy a Citroen that was to be waiting for them when they arrived in Paris. In good time they arrived at 2:30 p.m. October 18 on an Air France flight from Boston and claimed their automobile. Assured that such a purchase would have been impossible without a long wait if arranged in France, Gleeson was amazed and amused by the means taken to assure them an instant delivery on arrival. Father Convert, a European, took over the tasks of driving the car and translating when necessary for his bishop and the resident student-priest invited to accompany them on their tour.

They had planned their itinerary so they could be present for both the Centenary at Lourdes and the Marian Year celebrations in Rome. Unfortunately Pope Pius XII was ill; yet, in spite of ill health, he appeared for the solemnities in St. Peters. Traveling as tourists the three priests attended the activities in Rome, but made no attempt to request a personal visit with the Pope. To fulfill the primary reason for the journey Bishop Gleeson presented the ad limina reports and then the group continued their tour. They went as far south in Italy as Naples, then north and west to Lourdes.

At Lourdes they enjoyed the Centennial festivities before crossing the Pyrenees Mountains, to visit the families of Jesuit priests working in Alaska: Loyens from Belgium, Linssen and Baltussen from Holland. Everywhere they stopped, they received a warm welcome. The hospitality, at their Jesuit houses and the houses of Jesuit families, the good weather, and the spectacular scenery made it a memorable month. At its end Father Convert stayed to visit his parents in France and Bishop Gleeson returned to the United States.

On the flight home, he savored their good fortune in obtaining the car. That satisfaction became storytelling material when he heard that Father Convert sold the car before he left France for only $300 less than the purchase price. It is possible that the bishop told that story at the meetings in Washington, D.C. and Chicago before he set off for Fairbanks.

His arrival home on December 1 gave him sufficient time to rest before he officiated for a Solemn Pontifical Mass to close the Marian Year on December 8, 1954. Afterward he made a quick trip to Nenana and returned to Fairbanks for a December 13 consultation with the school building board on money-raising for the high school and Sisters' convent. Estimates for this project stood at $350,000. To obtain a $200,000 loan from a St. Louis bank, they needed $150,000 on hand. The board decided to contact, during January, those who were not fulfilling their pledges to the building fund.

The evening of the thirteenth, at the invitation of Army Chaplain James F. Madden, the bishop attended a Holy Name Society meeting at Ladd Air Force Base. His address to the airmen on the subject of the Alaskan missions was well received. Most of these men saw Alaskan villages from the air and had little knowledge concerning the life of the villagers.

Soon afterward he went back to Nenana where, in his capacity as pastor, he had several mission churches to visit. He now had Father Nevue's survey to direct his attempts to help the people. The towns that he endeavored to visit regularly were those on the railroad that had mission churches—Curry, Cantwell, Healy, Suntrana, Usibelli, McKinley Park. At Suntrana he received the best reception and accomplished the most. Several Catholic families and some Catholic single men resided at the coal mine.

DECISIONS AND CHANGES: 1955

A week and two days into 1955, Bishop Gleeson was hospitalized with a bout of indigestion. Another attack came on the twenty-first and again on the twenty-fourth. However, he felt well enough on January 23 to host an emergency meeting of his consultors at the Northward Building in Fairbanks. The Very Reverend Henry Schultheis, the new Provincial of the Oregon Province, and Fathers O'Connor, Anable, Spils, Donohue, Convert, Buchanan, and Conwell were present. That first day they met in the afternoon only. In the evening a public reception, arranged by Mrs. Joseph M. Ribar in honor of the visiting priests, was held in the parish hall from seven to nine.

The House Diary for the Vicariate records these conclusions of the bishop's consultation with his advisors:

...the chief result was a decision to close the boarding school at Holy Cross and to expand the Copper Valley School. The project was to include Indians from the entire interior. If possible, a Sisters' day school will continue at Holy Cross. Target date for the change to Copper Valley, September 1, 1956.

Chief objective of the new mission school will be education, not sheltering, of the unfortunate. Plans include a grade school, and a high school embracing both classical studies and trade school and domestic science.

Between now and the opening date, preschool children and others at Holy Cross not qualified for education will be returned to their villages or otherwise placed with families. Cooperation of the Welfare Department will be sought.

In effect the new school, with expanded facilities, would continue and expand the traditions of Holy Cross. It would also invite a mixed ethnic group to enable its students to learn the customs and cope with the ways of various peoples. It was a good solution, in its way; however, it did not take into account the dream Father Buchanan had nurtured, and it is the first indication that some children could be left behind in the name of quality education.

At approximately the same time as the meeting of the consultors, eleven missionaries from all corners of Alaska converged to make the first priests' retreat in the Vicariate. From January 27 through February 4 the men fed on spiritual inspiration from Father Mark Gaffney, S.J. They also had a wonderful time becoming better acquainted (some had never met), swapping stories, and benefiting from the experiences and insights of their peers. Jesuits had worked for many years in virtual isolation. This was now being perceived as an unnecessary deprivation on this "most difficult mission." Also, a territory grows and strengthens through uniformity, and uniformity becomes greater from the sharing and contact of its leaders. This was a move in that direction.

Two stories undoubtedly shared by the priests on this retreat had to do with community cooperatives. One, the reindeer herding being done at Father Fallert's mission in Stebbins and Father's hope that the project would become a stable economic occupation. Herding was not a new venture, just one that was lasting longer this time and, therefore, raising the hope that it would endure. Two, the cooperative electrical venture Father Fox installed in Mountain Village on the Yukon. Both projects received the blessing and help of the bishop as a means by which the Church could assist the people to live better lives in a world invaded by the white man. These cooperative ventures preceded the experiments that received a great deal of publicity after Vatican Council II.

A Clinical Health Review for the Bishop

Problems with indigestion had plagued Bishop Gleeson for many years. He had routinely blamed foreign menus and cooking. This latest illness in January could not be attributed to the food and therefore convinced him to arrange for a month-long evaluation at a clinic in Seattle. He scheduled it to take place in March.

In spite of his ill health, he implemented important steps before going to the clinic. He organized a working staff for Copper Valley construction. He appointed Father Buchanan as Superior with the added duty of obtaining donations of supplies, and Michael Collins, Buchanan's Jesuit assistant, to expedite delivery of materials from Anchorage to Copper Valley. He recruited Father Spils, with his team from St. Mary's to build the plans of Ned Abrams of Seattle. Eventually, Father Fox was to join the Copper Valley workers and supervise the Anchorage warehouse and the procurement of local sale items, particularly military overstocks. On another front Bishop Gleeson gave his official approval to the reinstatement of reindeer herds at Stebbins as an experimental cooperative venture toward Native economic independence. Shortly after giving these permissions, he left for Seattle on March 16 for a thorough clinical examination to determine the reasons for his indigestion and lowered resistance to local ailments.

Doctors agreed that the testing revealed diabetes and its attendant difficulties. At the conclusion of the examination, Bishop Gleeson said,

I had several disabilities. I thought it would be good to make preparation for succession and not have them waiting for a year or two like they did between my time and the death of my predecessor; so, I asked to have a coadjutor instead of an

auxiliary because a coadjutor has right of succession and no wait.

With the bishop at the clinic, Father Conwell's news letter for March 17, 1955 said that a bill authorizing school bus transportation had passed the Alaska Legislature. This was a boon for the Catholic Schools of Fairbanks. He also said that Fathers Buchanan and Collins had an apartment in Anchorage that would serve as the headquarters for the Copper Valley School Project. Another building, a warehouse, had been purchased previously to house mission building supplies. A last welcome item for all the missions said that Mrs. Samuel J. Balurdo of New York and her group of women, had offered to make silk articles for the missions: ciborium veils, tabernacle veils, burses, copes, and so on.

The Bishop Revitalized

Returning from Seattle on April 22, the bishop immediately plunged into work. His first major pen stroke approved Father O'Connor's request for permission to run for election as a delegate to the State Constitutional Convention. Then, resuming the mission rounds, the bishop went to Dillingham to assess with Father Endal the cost of rebuilding his burned out church and school. Reassured that it could be done with the help of insurance, Bishop Gleeson gave his consent.

At home again for Ascension Thursday, May 19, he presided at Immaculate Conception Baccalaureate ceremonies, and then at the Sacrament of Confirmation in the parish. Two weeks later he confirmed six children at St. Theresa's in Nenana. Father Conwell assisted at the ceremony that may have been the first of its kind in Nenana.

Before the bishop left Nenana to cook at Copper Valley, he provided for the spiritual needs of his missions down the highway. To take care of these parishes, the bishop appointed Father Nevue from Immaculate Conception in Fairbanks to substitute for him. Only then did Gleeson leave to cook at the Copper Valley construction site on the Tazlina River.

On June 9 he donned his chefs apron to cook for a month. Good weather made it possible for him to watch Father Spils use some very different methods from those used at St. Mary's. Here Father raised prefabricated walls, possibly the first time that the technique was used in Alaska. Then, Air Force steel webbing meant for runways was laid as reinforcement for the concrete flooring, and concrete blocks, manufactured on the Copper River site at much less expense than those commercially produced, finished the building process.

Precisely at the end of a month of cooking, on July 10, Chef Gleeson turned in his apron and went to Fairbanks to ready himself for a Confirmation ceremony at Eielson on the next day. Seventy-nine candidates were Confirmed. Not long after, he heard that Air Force steel webbing had disappeared from the surplus supply warehouses possibly, as some Jesuits suggested, Jake Spils' ingenuity influenced military building.

Expansion in Fairbanks

With a grade school opened and a high school planned in Fairbanks, it was time to think about a residence building for Jesuit faculty members. Using his own funds, on July 20 the bishop purchased an unfinished building in Slatersville (A subdivision on the edge of Fairbanks) for $4500. Remodeled, it would become known as Loyola Hall, a residence for the bishop and his chancellor, as well as for the Jesuit faculty and staff and visiting clergy that the parish house could not accommodate. The majority of the priests moved from Immaculate Conception parish house into the newly purchased and remodeled Loyola Hall. It followed that the hospital Sisters ceased to serve daily meals to the priests.

Content that his priests had a place to live, the bishop rode to Haines with Father Babb en route to Juneau for the Golden Jubilee celebration on July 29 of Father Joseph McElmeel. The veteran Alaska missionary had introduced Bishop Gleeson to air travel, and the two had been good friends ever since.

Unhappily, a school board meeting in Fairbanks on the first of August curtailed Gleeson's enjoyment of the anniversary party.

He hurried back to Fairbanks where he learned that the Fairbanks Exploration Company (FEC) had reneged on its agreement to sell the land and house used by its manager. Reluctantly, the bishop began to think of Loyola Hall as a convent for the Sisters. There was a collective Jesuit sigh of relief when he received word two days later that the Sisters would continue living at the hospital until a residence could be provided for them. No longer under pressure to provide a convent, the bishop approved the school board proposals for the enlargement of the grade school and the building of a high school. Bids went out on the third of August.

On schedule that September Monroe High School accepted its first class, limited to thirty students, in the ninth grade. Again, the children attended classes in the parish hall, but this time they had the satisfaction of watching their new school being built a few blocks away. Reverend Bernard McMeel was the first principal of the school, and priests of the parish and a layman comprised the teaching staff.

Meanwhile, the Sacred Congregation for the Oriental Church in Rome, sent Father Vsevelod Roshko (also spelled Rochkau and Rochcau) to Alaska where he began work on Little Diomede Island. Father Endal in Dillingham had requested a priest with Eastern Rite faculties more than five years before to assist with work among the Russian Orthodox people. Now, in the summer of 1955, he had arrived in Nome.

The Church and Statehood Politics

Ever an astute businessman Bishop Gleeson kept a sharp eye on the Alaska business and political scene. He believed that Alaska would never prosper until there was self-government and revenues to maintain it and that the Church could not attain fiscal stability until the people of Alaska could prosper. Very much aware that monopoly business interests fought against every bid for statehood, he monitored the movement by young political leaders to organize a Constitutional Convention for statehood. The clergy as a whole followed the political maneuvering with great interest.

Bishop Gleeson gave permission for Father O'Connor's name to appear on the election ballot for delegates to the state constitutional convention. Father, for more than ten years, was known and respected as head of the Alaska Housing Authority. This was a five-member group set up by the Territorial legislature. It had a fifteen-million-dollar revolving fund for a forty-year period placed at its disposal to implement the Alaska Housing Act. In the ten years Father steered the group, they had replaced more than seven hundred tarpaper shacks and

231

lean-to's with five room homes and modern facilities. Nevertheless, he lost his bid for a delegate seat.

In the midst of this convention excitement and practically on the eve of the Alaska State Constitutional Convention Bishop Charles D. White, D.D. of Spokane died. Bishop White had been co-consecrator for Bishop Gleeson ten years before. Now, Gleeson dropped everything and hurried to Spokane for the funeral. He remained for the installation of Spokane's new bishop, Bernard J. Topel on October 8. Then he went to Boise, Idaho for the Confraternity of Christian Doctrine Convention, on the weekend of October 9 through 11. There he presided at the General Lay Session on Monday, October 10. The aim of the meeting was to present information of interest and value to all interested in the vital problem of religious instruction for every age group.

Though Bishop Gleeson was quiet and self-effacing, he extended himself in many directions of which this attendance at the CCD convention is but an example. Letters of gratitude for advice and direction exist from Lewiston parishioners, service chaplains, prisoners, government agencies and political office holders.

While the bishop was away, Alaska politics commenced its historic processes. Father Boileau gave the Benediction on October 8, 1955 when the State Constitutional Convention came to order in the University of Fairbanks gymnasium. Beginning in October the elected convention members drafted and approved in seventy-five working days a constitutional document of 14,400 words. The constitution provided for a governor, a bicameral legislature, and a unified judicial system along with other needed components for a future state. In spite of these proceedings, Congress refused to seat Alaska's delegates and the next three years saw intense lobbying for statehood by the delegates and interested Alaskans.

While the convention was in session Father McMeel, principal of Monroe High School, organized a Newman Club among the university student body, and by the time the bishop arrived back in Fairbanks after the United States Bishops Conference political agitation had run its course. Within a week Gleeson went to Nenana for the first time since September and served his parishioners until the twenty-sixth when he departed for Fairbanks. There he stayed in Loyola Hall, the new faculty house.

THE LAST YEARS AS VICAR APOSTOLIC

The bishop prepared a special dinner and served the seven Jesuits at Loyola Hall on New Years Day 1956. Afterward they relaxed and enjoyed each other's company, a treat in itself, before work resumed. Early in the year the bishop made several visits to Nenana to prepare a group of children for first Holy Communion, and at Immaculate Conception parish he Confirmed a large group made up of parishioners, recent converts and people from Ladd and Eielson. As usual he began mission visitations and arranged the dates to allow him to open the meeting with his consultors. This year the meeting began on the eleventh and twelfth of February as scheduled.

The major issue on the consultors' agenda was a review of the accounting forms for the priests of the Vicariate. When these were reviewed and accepted, remaining business was completed in record time allowing the bishop to arrive back in Fairbanks for the closing days of the Alaska State Constitutional Convention at the University of Alaska. The constitutional document was considered the best ever produced for a state, and the bishop with Fathers Boileau and Conwell attended the signing ceremony on February 16 at 2:00 in the afternoon. Bishop Gleeson closed the assembly with a Benediction.

National sentiment strongly favored statehood at this time and Sam Rayburn, Speaker of the House, dropped his opposition to the bill.

Between frequent visits to Nenana and Copper Valley, and his annual visits to the missions, the bishop was seldom at home until April first, Easter Sunday. On this day he was in Nenana to say Mass for his people and remained available to them. His availability was fortunate because the military announced that it was clearing its Anchorage warehouse of wartime supplies. Brother Feltes must have made a strong case when he sought permission to stock military building materials for Copper Valley because the bishop purchased a building in Anchorage suitable for use as a supply center and a Jesuit residence. Drivers from the Air Force Transport Division and other volunteers working on their free time or vacation time began moving the stores to Copper Valley using the worn Buchanan pickup, donated military trailers, other used vehicles, and a new truck contributed by Bing Crosby.

Copper Valley School Construction

Construction of the school now accelerated. Both amateur and professional people from Fairbanks, Valdez, Anchorage, and local homes made up volunteer work crews. Father Spils was head of the construction crew that he brought with him from the St. Mary's project. That core building crew consisted of George Sipary and his wife Alice, and George's brother, Anthony and his wife, Rita, and their children, Simeon and Elizabeth, Eskimos from St. Mary's, and Henry Kobuk from St. Michael on the Bering Sea. Others on the crew were: volunteers from Copper Center; Nulato; Fort Yukon; Worcester, Massachusetts; Gonzaga University and Gonzaga High; Phoenix, Arizona; and New York. On weekends this basic crew was often augmented by as many as twenty Holy Name men from Elmendorf Airforce Base at Anchorage.

The goal was to open the school in September and Buchanan's dream school/university was taking shape, but not as he had dreamed of it. He told a writer for The Catholic Digest,

I'm not worried. If I sometimes do find myself feeling a little low, I look up at those mountains around us, and I tell myself, Who am I to worry? If He who could make these mountains wants this school He will see that it gets built.

The overall result from the unmatched materials they used was pleasing enough to confound the critics. It reflected the faith of the builders, faith that began with Bishop Gleeson who confidently relied on volunteer labor and donations. More accurately, it began with the faith of Father Buchanan who planned, though he had no materials, then begged major portions of his needs. His faith spread to procurers, shoppers for bargains and gifts, and continued even to the builders and their use of imagination and ingenuity to raise an aesthetically acceptable structure.

The Seattle <u>Northwest</u> <u>Progress</u> newspaper in an article on the school reported that $3,000,000 in gifts of cement, lumber, steel, aluminum, pipe and construction equipment came from corporations and industries in the contiguous United States. Some of those companies also supplied materials for the four chapels previously built. For instance: Park River Lumber Company of Sandpoint, Idaho supplied 100,000 feet of lumber; Alaska Freight Lines gave free transport from Seattle to Alaska; West Coast Freight Lines and Helphrey Freight Lines carried from Idaho to Seattle.

When the September 1956 opening date was announced, Father Spils knew that construction would have to be completed while classes were in session. Every aspect of preparation was speeded up. In June 1956, Holy Cross children chosen to attend the new school were notified; others were assured that Holy Cross would continue as a day school as long as possible. Father Buchanan and Sister George Edmond, Superior at Holy Cross and subsequently at Copper Valley, panicked until they were assured that a group of instructors,

Jesuits and Sisters of Saint Ann, would accompany the children to the new school.

Monroe Foundation of Fairbanks

Along with thoughts of Copper Valley and its opening, Bishop Gleeson was preoccupied with the development of the Monroe Foundation of Fairbanks, Alaska, Inc. Founded for the *purpose of establishing an endowment fund the Foundation aimed to provide gifts, scholarships and loans to the educational organization.* Its first large money-raising function was a dinner slated for June 20, 1956. The dinner, conceived as an elegant social affair, drew five hundred people from all over Alaska and from all walks of life including a good sprinkling of politicians. Foundation members took this diversity of support as evidence of a general appreciation for the work of the Church. To their delight, the proceeds paid off the Fairbanks school debt.

Still flushed with the dinner's success, the Catholic community feted Archbishop William J. O'Brien, President of the Catholic Church Extension Society, when he came to Alaska on July 21. In the words of Bishop Gleeson, his presence was "a delicate compliment." The Extension Society had contributed many hundreds of thousands of dollars to church building over the preceding eight years. Perhaps the Archbishop was curious about this territory that was being so generously supplied. Bishop O'Flanagan accompanied Archbishop O'Brien to Fairbanks and Bishop Gleeson, and Father Boileau met them at the International Airport.

A month later, on August 20, the bishop participated in a Rosary rally at Griffin Baseball Park in Fairbanks. Captain Schumacker from Ladd Air Field gave the welcoming address and thanked the bishop for bringing Father Peyton. The bishop spoke briefly and then Father Peyton, himself, gave an address and presided at Benediction of the Blessed Sacrament.

While the Crusade was progressing in Fairbanks, Sister Antoinette left St. Mary's after twenty-years of service. She had helped to plan St. Mary's and oversaw the move from Akulurak. Also, her Sisters at St. Mary's say that it was through her efforts that the Little Sisters came to Alaska. Sister left the mission with little fanfare and just missed Father Peyton's arrival at St. Mary's by two days. The bishop and his well-known guest departed immediately after the Rosary ceremonies and conferring of the Sacrament of Confirmation. However, before the bishop left, he appointed Father Fallert as head of the school at Copper Valley. Then the bishop proceeded to St. Michael mission and on to Fairbanks. He arrived home in good time for the dedication of the new Catholic high school.

The new high school and cornerstone were blessed on September 1, 1956 after Bishop Gleeson officiated at an out of doors Mass of the Holy Ghost. At these ceremonies Father Conwell was Master of Ceremonies and Father Boileau gave the dedication address. Jim McNealy and Danny Koudelka acted as servers. The official name, Monroe High School, was bestowed in honor of Father Francis M. Monroe, S.J. who had established Fairbanks first Catholic Church in 1904. The celebrations continued until the school year officially began on September 6.

Many of the guests at the Monroe High School dedication were actively interested in the progress being made at Copper Valley where three buildings were roofed and three others were under construction. The deadline for the opening of the Copper Valley School had been postponed from September to October. Nevertheless, expert builders continued in awe of Father Spils ability to produce constant construction with a crew that varied from nine to over thirty volunteers, and materials that came haphazardly as they were donated or shippers managed to deliver.

A few faculty had come early to prepare living quarters and classrooms. One of these was Sister Mary Agatha (Jeannette LaRose) who had come from Pius X Mission in Skagway. One afternoon she was intent upon finding furnishings for the main room of the wooden building. *At the moment it was designated as her future classroom but was being used,* she said, *as a dining room three times a day, as a recreation room for the staff during the evening, and as a storeroom for dry staples.* In her quest for the furnishings Sister had learned to crawl under tarps spread over accumulated building supplies or surplus materials. This day she found enough tables, though one was minus a leg, so smiling a most satisfied smile, she emerged from under a dusty canvas to find herself looking up at Bishop Gleeson who had just arrived from Fairbanks.

The bishop wore fatigue trousers and a checked shirt. Sister's coif was dirty and her work apron ready for the laundry, but she was triumphant. To the bishop's, *How's everything?* she responded triumphantly, *Fine, bishop! But we don't have water and we have no Blessed Sacrament.* His face lit up as he unhesitatingly responded, *I can give you God, but God will have to give you water.*

Mid October arrived and the school was ready to receive the children from Holy Cross giving Father Buchanan a problem. He needed to bring the children from the west bank of the Yukon River over approximately five hundred miles of mountains and semi-frozen tundra to the confluence of the Tazlina and Copper Rivers. Nelson David, then president of Alaska Airlines, responded to Father's needs with an airlift. He charted a route from McGrath Air Field through a mountain pass for three small

Stinson bush planes with a passenger capacity of three to five people.

"Operation Snowbird" pilots took off on October 14 from an improvised strip of eight hundred feet on a frozen, snowy sandbar in the Yukon River with their load of youngsters. The airlift went on for hours before the thirty-five children their teachers and luggage were transported. Each takeoff and landing was a perilous event. Once in the air they had a forty-two mile shuttle south to Aniak, where a four-engine Alaska DC4 Starliner waited to take them to Copper Valley. For the children especially, it was an unforgettable experience. The school opened with eighty students and a staff consisting of Father Fallert, the Sisters of St. Ann, Jesuit Scholastics and lay volunteers.

At Copper Valley the youngsters found a spirit wholly unlike that of Holy Cross. There existed no regimentation, no segregation of boys and girls during the school day. There was plenty of food and freedom of movement. Housekeeping duties were much lighter, consisting mostly of keeping their quarters in order. There was neither woodcutting nor wood-hauling duty, no garden or kitchen work. Doors from the school exited to trails into the woods, to the river, or to the road. There were, of course, safety rules, but the feeling of freedom overrode all.

Back at Holy Cross, spirits were low that day, and the religious left behind remembered when the school was new, easy to keep up, useful and capable of long years of service. That was almost seventy years before. That day four priests, three sisters, and one Brother remained there to service a handful of pupils from the neighboring villages. For those who keep score, 153 missionaries worked there. Some spent many years, some just a short time, but all were dedicated and loved the people and the place. Brother Aloysius B. Laird was one Jesuit deeply affected by the closing of the boarding school because he neither stayed behind nor went with the children. He went to Fairbanks to be custodian at Monroe High School.

On his way back from the Bishops' meeting in Washington, Gleeson stopped at Copper Valley, perhaps to resolve the quiet upset among the faculty. Not everyone respected Father Fallert's position as Superior when the Principal of the school was absent. Though the Jesuits were most affected, any such one-on-one conflict disrupts the whole, even the students. At any rate the bishop continued from Copper Valley to Fairbanks where he was once again home to celebrate Christmas with his brother Jesuits.

For the children acclimating themselves at CVS, the faculty realized that a trip to Anchorage, Valdez, or Fairbanks brought them into contact with people from many backgrounds and

243

walks of life. Restaurants, doctors' offices, stores, and other schools gave a new meaning to table manners, social amenities and dress codes. Words foreign to the bush, like "parade" and "competition", became part of a living vocabulary.

Competition, so important to the white man, was a difficult concept for these children. As an example, when the ski team entered a cross-country interscholastic competition in Anchorage, Copper Valley skiers allowed the others to pass, enjoyed the beauty of the course, and jaunted off on side trips wherever interest lured them. Finally, having returned to the starting point hours after everyone else, they could not understand why people had worried about them. It was still light. What was the hurry? Far more interested in playing the game than in competitive rivalry, the children took sportsmanship awards year after year rather than championship cups.

Academically and socially each year students attained more insight, more confidence in their ability to cope in white society, more sophistication enabling graduates to successfully attend university classes or vocational schools. In later years many of these students went on to become teachers, lawyers, mayors in their communities, leaders in Native corporations, owners of businesses, and highly skilled industrial technologists. Buchanan's dream for the Native children was blooming.

This social development of the student body depended upon a dedicated maintenance and teaching staff. One of the original volunteers at Copper Valley Sschool, Al Gyllenhammer, known as Gill, did anything that needed doing from driving trucks and working surplus in Anchorage to cleaning debris on the property. That was in 1956 when the small faculty needed every bit of help they could get just to keep the floors clean. Father Spils thanked God for willing and competent extra hands. The following years would prove that other volunteers were equally dedicated.

VOLUNTEERS: 1957

Early in January Father Boileau hired a cook for the Loyola residence and the bishop, after a trip to Nome, began living in Nenana. It was some time since he had lived there, but he continued as pastor who arranged to have others fill-in when he was busy elsewhere. He did travel to Fairbanks frequently especially during three weeks of February when Father Conwell was hospitalized. Otherwise he continued his regular routine of hosting visitors, writing letters, visiting his mission stations on the highway out of Nenana and the other far-flung missions in the Vicariate. He also kept in close touch with the work in Copper Valley. One of his very few extant writings was an article for "Extension Magazine" written during this time.

In March Father Henry J. Schultheis, Provincial, from Portland, Father Edmund A. Anable, Mission Procurator from Seattle, and Father John P. Fox from Holy Cross came to Fairbanks and Nenana for a visit. They then joined Father Conwell to drive down to Copper Valley for the annual consultors' meeting. At Copper Valley they found the school in session with grade and high school Indian, Eskimo and white students using the three finished spokes of the projected seven. A fully operational construction camp was in full swing

246

working in the roofed fourth spoke and preparing for the building of the fifth wing. As the three-day meeting opened on March 5, hopes were very high and interest even higher.

The first order of business was the dedication of the school. This ceremony marked the date at which the institution became officially Copper Valley School (CVS) and the Fathers gave the naming thoughtful consideration. It was already the home of approximately seventy students, two-thirds Eskimo and Indian. That number was considered just a little more than one-third its intended size. About one-half of the students were in the elementary grades and the remainder in the high school. Because of the unique ethnic mix among the students and the tremendous publicity given the project, there were many visitors. At one point in time tour buses stopped at the school.

Bishop Gleeson and Fathers Anable, Hargreaves, Cunningham and Fox returned to Fairbanks after the meeting. Within a day Father Anable would be on a plane to his office in Seattle, and Hargreaves and Cunningham back to their stations in the bush. Father Fox planned a week of retreat before returning to Holy Cross. The bishop, too, would be away visiting missions until early May when he was scheduled to preside at a Monroe High School/Immaculate Conception joint assembly. The students from grades five through high school attended the assembly in the new high school gymnasium to honor those receiving awards for excellence. With the bishop presiding a ceremony honored the Knights of the Altar, and the principal, Father McMeel, announced various high school awards and prizes.

Shortly thereafter, Michael Stepovich was invited to Loyola Hall with his wife and five oldest children to attend Mass and enjoy a breakfast prepared by the bishop. Even the young people, well aware of Bishop Gleeson's reputation as an outstanding cook, eagerly accepted the invitation. The occasion was a celebration for the Territorial Governor-elect. The breakfast predated the inauguration ceremonies that Father Conwell would attend the next month through the generosity of one of his parishioners. While the group ate, they undoubtedly conversed about the admission of Alaska to the union. Everything pointed to possible entry very soon. Alaskans expected the House Interior and Insular Affairs Committee to recommend admission momentarily. However, in true Washington style, consideration by the House deferred the vote for another year.

The Stepovich children enjoyed pride of family for their father the Governor-elect; the Copper Valley students enjoyed pride of class for their first graduates in June of 1957. To add to the prestige of the graduation ceremonies, Bishop Gleeson celebrated a Pontifical High Mass and then attended the commencement exercises. Jesuit Father Wilfred P. Schoenberg, S.J., of Gonzaga Prep further honored the class by his attendance. He was in Fairbanks to search out material for the province historical archives and returned to Fairbanks with the bishop and Brother Laird after the rejoicing.

Sister George Edmond, Principal of Copper Valley School, however, flew to Massachusetts for a vacation. There she came into contact with a volunteer organization at Regis College that prompted her to telephone Bishop Gleeson for permission to invite volunteers to Alaska. He thought it a wonderful idea, and suggested that he pay any volunteers a monthly stipend of ten dollars as well as transportation. Although the Regis' plan was primarily intended to serve the southwest area of the United States, the coordinator agreed to inform prospective volunteers of the needs at Copper Valley. That year five women took up the challenge to work in Alaska at an unfinished boarding school for Native children during subzero winters, with camping conditions for living, interior finishing work after teaching hours, cultural differences between themselves and the children and among the children themselves, and a no-pay understanding.

All five women were twenty-one years old and newly graduated. Four came from colleges in Massachusetts; namely, Regis College in Weston, and Anna Marie College in Worcester,

249

and one from Rhode Island. In addition, Steve Jankowski, a thirty-year-old welder, came from Massachusetts. He subsequently stayed for ten years.

That same year, 1957, the Jesuit Scholastic John Morris joined the faculty and a carload of young people from Gonzaga University joined the Copper Valley staff. This influx of enthusiastic young teachers and Gonzaga university youths solved the staffing problem for Sister George Edmond. At the same time, the innovative volunteer movement was established in Alaska.

The movement spread by word of mouth and the bishop screened and placed people as they came from eastern United States, and from Spokane's Gonzaga University and its feeder communities. Unfortunately, he neither took the time to shape a program, nor to set time limits for volunteer applicants or for missionary requests for help; nor did he send adequate informative correspondence. In fact, he did not take into account that these people would need some lead time to prepare financially and socially for leaving home, and that they should be oriented before taking a position in such a difficult place. As a consequence, problems arose. Several people received an acceptance a few days before they needed to be at their destination, and for some, the name of the destination and of the priest expecting them was the extent of their preparation. For a while Father Spils' nephew and his friends attempted to orient the volunteers and prepare them for the culture shock they would encounter. However, volunteers began increasing in number and the Gonzaga young people working to orient them could no longer cope.

The following year, 1958, volunteers who had worked at Copper Valley School organized and called themselves Lay Apostolate Mission Boosters. Their purpose as stated by Melvin Kayes, reads: **LAMB is an organization of former lay apostles in the Alaska mission fields. Our principal task is to recruit and screen Catholic young people with a college degree to teach in the Alaska missions.**

The LAMB organization worked very effectively and volunteers, though seldom given widespread recognition, did a great deal for the missions in Alaska. In time, a brochure was prepared and sent out by LAMB. They provided a much-needed work giving help to bewildered volunteers. It was estimated that the volunteers saved the missions about $600,000 in approximately twenty years.

In spite of the haphazard organization and sometimes-chaotic results, the volunteer Apostolate flourished and spread its roots across Alaska for the next seven years. Then, in 1964, the bishop gave the task of volunteer recruitment to Father Boileau who promptly placed it in the hands of Father John J.

Morris, S.J. Father Morris, had watched the growth of the project since 1957 when he was on the faculty of Copper Valley School as a Scholastic. His observations prompted him to show Father Boileau a recruitment plan that he thought would benefit the LAMB effort.

Two years later, September 1966, the Very Reverend Father Provincial proposed that an agency be set up in the office of the Jesuit Missions in Portland to prepare Lay Volunteers for work in the missions of the Province. Bishop Gleeson understood the assistance such an office would be to the recruiting of volunteers; therefore, after appending two conditions, he approved the proposal.

His conditions stipulated that a candidate for a position in Alaska be referred to him for assignment, and that financial arrangements with those people coming to Alaska be made by himself. Both conditions assumed that the bishop would be the person to know the needs and financial status of the diocese.

Being confined to an office in Portland did not appeal to Father Morris; nevertheless, he moved into an office, and proceeded to set up his program for recruitment, screening and orientation. Renamed, the enterprise became the Jesuit Volunteer Corps, popularly known as JVC. Its members and their spirit can be found throughout the United States.

Father Baud's Anniversary

That summer of 1957 Bishop Gleeson traveled to Nulato to attend Father Baud's twenty-fifth anniversary of ordination as a priest on June 20. Wilfred Schoenberg wrote a bit about Father Baud in The Oregon Jesuit. He said that the anniversary was an historic occasion because more than two priests came together in the interior of Alaska. In this case Bishop Gleeson, Fathers Henry Hargreaves, himself and three other priests had gathered at Nulato. He then went on to say that the meeting was richly merited as Father John Baptist Baud had spent twenty-two of his twenty-five priestly years in the interior of Alaska with the Tena Indians along the Yukon. In the winter, temperatures reached nearly seventy below zero, but Father Baud said that he likes it there, so he hasn't been outside more than once in all those years.

In his description Father Schoenberg went on to say, Father speaks a delightful English with a French dialect and overtones of the Yukon dialect. His personality is warm and full of exuberance. Though he claims to be nothing and know little, he built the priest house, did beautiful paintings of the mission and surrounding mountains and Native life, made puppets and a stage for them, printed photographs and varnished floors, and took care of his peoples' temporal and spiritual needs.

253

About Bishop Gleeson's part in the celebration Father takes it upon himself to poke a little fun:

I remember going with a crowd of the Indian people, up to the airport which was on top of the hill, to meet the Bishop's plane. I grabbed some boughs to keep the mosquitoes off. The Bishop got out of the plane and he sure looked like he was just off of Ellis Island. He had on a leather coat that was tacky; his collar was shiny. He just looked really tacky.

Baud's house was shiny clean. About seven o'clock in the evening, I was asked to go and hear confessions. I said, "Sure, I'd be glad to do that while Hargreaves, the Bishop, and Baud powwowed." I got out about 11:30. When I got to the house, the three of them were sitting there and they said to me, "We have decided that you are to preach tomorrow." I said, "Hey, wait a minute, you're the Bishop; you're here for this occasion; you should preach, not I." And he just looked at me, straight. He didn't flinch. He just looked at me. Straight. He said, "No, you're going to preach tomorrow."

So, I got up there, and the general tenure of the sermon was: Father Baud has spent twenty-five years working at this place. Here in the whole district there are seven hundred fifty people. In Central America there is one priest for eighteen thousand people. They can't get to the sacraments. Those people want a priest and here we have a priest for a little handful of people. How many show-up for Mass? How many go to the sacraments? How many help with this mission? He has a bad heart and he has to cut his own wood. What is the matter here?

The Bishop sat there, his eyes were watery, and he was watching me with great interest. He said to me afterwards, "You should come up here every year and go around to the missions and tell them all the same thing." I said, "Bishop, why don't you do it?" Then he drops the subject.

School Statistics

The following statistics came to the Bishop's attention at the beginning of the 1957-1958 school year. The list reads like a quick review of ten years work.

- Immaculate Conception School—354
- Copper Valley School—70 boarders;
- Holy Cross School—81 day students
- Oblates of Our Lady of the Snows—6
- The Lay Apostolate Program—31 volunteers
- Ninth year of intense building—under construction, McGrath, Newtok, Mountain Village.

And with this cheerful news, Bishop Gleeson and Father Conwell drove to Copper Valley to attend a school staff meeting after which the bishop went on to visit the missions on the

Bering Coast and the Yukon River. When he came back, he went to Eielson Air Force Base to present the papal medal "Benemerenti" to Colonel Ray Will, the base commander. He was an exemplary Catholic and truly deserved the medal. A Solemn Pontifical Mass and reception followed the presentation. Another presentation in October went to Father Paul O'Connor. The National Association for Housing and Redevelopment presented a citation to Father for his twelve years of service as Commissioner of the Alaska Housing Authority. During those years most of the poorest housing was replaced by new homes. Only the most outlying areas had not yet been renewed.

Coming off the last of his visits to the missions for 1957, the bishop prepared for his annual trip to Washington and the Extension meeting in Chicago. As was his custom he returned in early December just in time to greet Cardinal Spellman who was on a round-the-world tour of United States military bases. The Cardinal had visited Eielson and Ladd, but was unable to reach Barrow because his plane broke down. Taking advantage of the situation, Bishop Gleeson invited the Cardinal and his companions, Bishop O'Flanagan and several chaplains, to tour the new Immaculate Conception and Monroe High Schools. The guests were suitably impressed, especially with the new science laboratory and the newly inaugurated French language classes.

Finally, in the last week of December Father Conwell won, through a drawing, a free plane trip to his hometown. A local flower and gift shop donated the prize and the bishop improved on it by deciding that Father should take a ten day leave and fly to Spokane immediately so that he might be present for his mother's seventy-fifth birthday on January 3.

A TABOO DISCARDED: 1958

Preceding the consultors' February meeting, Father Segundo Llorente preached an Ignatian retreat for the group, and was rewarded for his preparations by enthusiastic praise. At least one retreatant said that it was one of the finest retreats ever given. *Good enough to be given the Holy Father.* Father modestly replied that it was just an Ignatian retreat with a Spanish accent.

The annual meeting that began on February 14 addressed and approved several important issues. The first was a consensus agreement that there should be a retreat for Jesuits in Alaska and a meeting of Jesuits in Alaska on alternate years, and that this gathering should take place in February. Another topic concerned a more workable form for the annual financial report sent to the bishop's office. Father Conwell pointed out that the forms in use included headings that did not conform to headings in account books required by the Procurator's office in Seattle. This resulted in confusion each year. Proposed new forms were discussed and approved pending the approval of the Procurator. Discussions continued about spending by individual priests for their individual needs and the bishop provided suitable answers.

The consultors also looked at the possibility of molding St. Mary's into a model village in charge of a priest. The possibility did not sit well with the bishop; however, he did not react visibly and the item was tabled for later consideration. Another item classified as old business brought some thoughtful, and some heated, discussion after Father James E. Poole spoke about the need for a strong radio station in Nome. He stressed the necessity for using up-to-date means of communication for Catholic teaching and pointed out the strong, active stations in use by Protestant groups. He also mentioned the possibility of Russian Communist radio programs and the impact they might have on Nome residents. No immediate action was taken on this question. The bishop, however, was aware that Father Poole could raise the needed funds.

James W. Plamondon presented a position paper, *Advisability of Planes for Missionaries.* All of the consultors were acquainted with the tragedy of 1930. Some were present when the first plane purchased for the missions and brought to Alaska by Brother Feltes crashed on October 12. The crash resulted in the instant death of Philip Delon, Superior of the Jesuit Missionaries in Alaska, William F. Walsh, a missionary to Kotzebue on loan from the Archdiocese of San Francisco, and Ralph Wien, a commercial pilot from Fairbanks. After the accident the use of planes was forbidden to the missionaries.

The minutes from this meeting record no real objections to the use, or at least the trial use, of planes. There were two effective points raised in their favor:

1. A missionary's plane could be equated with a pastor's automobile.

2. Schedules for bush flights were often unreliable and wasted much ministry time.

There was a considerable amount of discussion before all agreed that planes should be new, or practically new, and that training should be at a regular flying school. Discussion concluded, Gleeson announced that the time had come to experiment on a small scale, and the Provincial, Henry J. Schultheis, agreed that old fears should be put aside

Just seven months elapsed before Father Convert "picked up" in Fairbanks, Alaska, a second-hand plane for use on his mission at Kaltag for the satellite places of Unalakleet, Egvik, and neighboring villages. He took his technical training at the Tacoma School and Flying Service, in Washington. Bernard Oswald, a former Bellarmine student given tuition during the depression days, donated the training service as a form of in-kind repayment. If this experiment proved successful other missionaries would receive their wings, and planes would be purchased as the budget allowed. The phrase, as the budget allowed, was always a thorn for bishop and priests because funds were always low. Years later Father Convert confessed that the Provincial had urged him to push for planes; however, the minutes do not reflect any such "push".

After Father Plamondon sat down, Father Tom Cunningham explained and answered questions about "Operation Ice Skate", the project of the Geophysical Year. Father Tom had begun as a technical advisor; now the military gave him almost the last say on all things pertaining to camp and camp buildings, supplies, screening of personnel, and other project necessities. His choice of stable ice floes always remained good while the Russian project constantly changed sites.

Other topics addressed by the assembled priests concerned St. Mary's music program, and policies concerning student acceptance into the school. A leadership discussion took place, and then Father Greif introduced the topic of the Eastern Rite Mass. Father reminded everyone that Russian missionaries long had evangelized the Dillingham area before any Jesuits came to Alaska, and the Native converts to the Orthodox creed were steadfast in their loyalty. He went on to say that Father Wilcock, a Jesuit from Russian Center in New York, suggested that were Father Greif able to offer the Oriental liturgy, it would be possible to show the people, in a striking manner, that their religion is much like the Roman Rite. Then he went on to introduce the Rite before the bishop offered Mass. Father gave a running commentary during the Mass, and answered questions afterward.

There was great interest in the topic because Father Roshko, who had been ministering on Diomede Island, had recently founded an Eastern Rite mission on the grounds of Holy Rosary Mission in Dillingham, yet canonically independent. He was to serve the Russian Orthodox people in that area.

When the meeting concluded, its fifteen participants quickly dispersed to their various destinations. The bishop went first to Fairbanks and Nenana and then continued on some of his annual visitation of the missions until March, when he interrupted his rounds for a trip to Portland.

While the bishop and provincial were talking in Portland they discussed the thought that had been entertained about selling the church property in Nenana. At this meeting that idea was put to rest. Nenana would continue to be Mission Headquarters in Northern Alaska. Also while there, the two men discussed Father Anable's continuing troubled conscience about the bishop's fiscal policy. The two men examined the Jesuit regulations at length. In the end Father Schulthies wrote a letter to Father Anable assuring him that the bishop was solely in charge of all monies in the diocese, and Father was to stop worrying.

To help soothe Father Anable, the bishop wrote to Father Conwell directing him to pay off a loan Anable had taken from the bank. His letter also explained that a salmon shipment from St. Mary's had been flawed in its packing and part of Father Anable's financial troubles came from that mistake. Repacked the fish would soon be sold but at a loss of three dollars a case, possibly as many as a few thousand cases.

Within a short time another problem, this time caused by the Yukon River, made Father Anable grit his teeth as he paid for the bishop's solution. The difficulty:

- Shipping prices rose dramatically when the Yukon River shifted eastward and left a long silt and sand bar in front of Holy Cross so that barges could not approach the shore.
  The solution:
- A tug found in Nenana purchased at a reasonable price, and a barge with a large steel hull, found in McGrath also purchased.
- The tug reconditioned to make it a truly shallow draft vessel.
- Father Jack Wood and his father towed the barge on a very dangerous trip some two hundred miles to St. Mary's and made it fast to the tug.

All began well then the Native engineer from St. Mary's who brought the reconditioned barge to McGrath for loading received news that his little boy had drowned at St. Mary's. Like a good father, he left for home immediately. Troubles were not over. The pilot of the barge employed to thread the sandbars in the river was an alcoholic, and the second engineer died in a fire in his cabin. The next summer a priest from St. Mary's did transport two buildings down to the school, but the problems of barge ownership were greater than the benefits. The vessel was sold the following year.

At the meeting in Portland much business was accomplished before the participants turned to evening sports broadcasts. The bishop enjoyed the citywide excitement of Seattle University's race for the basketball championship while watching the games with the resident priests and joining in their lively conversations. Also, before flying to New York in pursuit of acquiring Sisters to serve in Alaska, he visited with the Toussaints who had lived next door to Loyola Hall in Fairbanks. Mr. Toussaint later told this story recounted by the bishop during the visit:

One of the Eskimo women in a village the bishop visited annually used to provide him with Eskimo dolls for money raisers or gifts. Usually she would send the dolls to him. This particular time he was visiting the village and she suggested that he take the dolls with him since he was on his way home. With a glint in his eye that always preceded a humorous remark the bishop said to her, "But I'm not supposed to travel with dolls!"

The New School Year

A staff meeting in September at Copper Valley put into writing the primary goal of the school in the following words: **Copper Valley School is designed to prepare the Native children to adjust to our way of life. We strive to train the more talented children recommended by our missionary Fathers.**

Successful school meetings had taken place in St. Mary's about that same time and all scholastic programs were prepared. St. Mary's, however, had a fish packing business that Father Anable had alluded to a few months earlier. Now, a letter to Father Poole, the principal, on October 10 resurrected the whole of the troubles about which Father Anable worried.

The St. Mary's cannery operation involved more than a packing accident. The fact that a local trader threatened to cut off villagers' credit if they did not work (fish) for him was a far greater worry. Father Anable suggested to the bishop that the Fathers set up cooperatives in the villages of St. Marys and Pilot Station to relieve the pressure. In reply, the bishop pointed out that the priests could not be involved in Native co-ops except as advisors. The problem remained to be solved;

however, this dilemma constituted a learning experience for the Eskimos.

As usual the year had been fraught with large problems many of which involved finances. The bishop's visits to the missions were heartening for him as he viewed new churches and chapels in the villages. Tens of thousands of dollars, contributed by various organization and associations enabled the priests and villagers to build anew or repair their parish buildings. Most of the contributions totaled $20,000 to $25,000 for each building and that sum covered most of the shipping costs for lumber shipped into the treeless tundra.

Traveling to Washington and Chicago the Vicar took his worries with him. This year, although he seemed to ignore the financial crunch and continued to seek out land for the erection of a greatly needed cathedral, chancery, and episcopal residence, building and paying ongoing maintenance costs was a consistent need about which he brooded. If only he could find a consistent way to raise money…

As was his custom, after the meetings in the east, he visited his relatives in Detroit. Usually, he broke his trip home with a stop in Seattle, and sometimes at places to which he had been invited. This year one of his stops was to make contact with Father Ralph E. Villwock of Martin, South Dakota, a knowledgeable fund-raiser. Their conversation impressed the bishop enough so that he invited Father to address the consultors at the February meeting in Alaska. When he continued toward home his burden was considerably lighter enabling him to bring smiles for the Christmas celebrations.

World Belligerence Alive in Alaska

The Vietnam War was making itself felt in unrest and aggressive speech and action in all segments of United States society. Many Alaskans funneled their belligerence into the political fight for statehood. At hearings in Washington, D.C. Father Bernard R. Hubbard, S.J., nationally known for his geological exploration in Alaska, spoke for the anti-statehood lobby. His popularity lent considerable weight to his words.

Refuting Father Hubbard's argument that Alaska needed much more development before it could support itself, Father Paul O'Connor of the Alaska Housing Commission, and Monsignor Edgar Gallant, principal of the Native children's school in Skagway, spoke for the Bishops, Gleeson and O'Flanagan, and the Roman Catholic clergy of Alaska. They pointed out that Father Hubbard did not live in Alaska, and, therefore, was not really in touch with the inhabitants of the territory. Moreover, they reasoned, Alaska would never flourish until it had its own revenues and self-government.

The issues were heatedly and sometimes bitterly debated by many factions, including the fishing interests based in Seattle. Finally, during the summer session of Congress in June 1958, the House voted in favor of Alaska's admission to the union, and the Senate cast its favorable vote on June 30, 1958. Six months later President Eisenhower formally admitted Alaska as the forty-ninth state on January 3, 1959. Until then, Arizona, in 1912, was the last state to be admitted.

Almost immediately, elections for the state legislature became the topic of interest for everyone in the new state.

A Year of Bad News: 1959

After the political excitement in January, the annual consultors' meeting was a quiet interlude. They revisited their determination to have an annual retreat and settled for a retreat on alternate years. New business included an address by Father Villwock. He spoke about a method for long-term money raising by initiating a letter campaign to be written under the Vicariate heading and signed by the bishop. The men promptly accepted the suggestion. They decided that the campaign would be inaugurated and handled out of the Seattle offices. Unfortunately, the mailing of the first The Alaskan Shepherd, written in Portland, was delayed for a year.

In April of 1959 the bishop, unable to wait any longer for results of the projected mail campaign, talked Father Anable into writing a distinctly Alaskan newsletter. Father had so often deplored the bishop's spending now found himself agreeing to the requested letter. They mailed The Alaskan Shepherd to about eighty people they both knew to be former generous donors. It came out with a letterhead from the Vicariate Apostolic of Alaska, 615 Betty Street, Fairbanks, Alaska, and over the bishop's signature, as suggested by Father Villwock.

The following quotation is from a copy of that letter.

Dear Friend:

You know great things are expected from Alaska! Given time these things can eventuate. The Church will also be expected to keep pace. In the Vicariate the missionary Fathers have worked long, hard years to promote the Faith. Pope Pius XI called these Alaskan Missions, "The most difficult in the world".

Conditions today are hardly less difficult. Consider that our people are scattered over an area nearly twice the size of Texas. About one-third are Indians, Eskimos and Aleuts. Their income is so small they cannot help much....

As the Vicar Apostolic of Alaska it is my job to try to provide for our Catholics here and to bring the blessings of our Holy Faith to others. Our needs are rather elemental. We have no

Cathedral nor Episcopal Palace and are not asking you to supply them. The need is for small churches, chapels and schools. We must provide housing for our Missionaries and their helpers. We must provide transportation for personnel and materials. We must expand our educational and Social Service facilities and train men and women for this essential work of the Missions. Imagine, if you can, what all of this means in terms of expense in this remote part of the world.

The letterhead confirms the use of a small house on Betty Street as a Vicariate office and residence for the bishop and his staff: Fathers William Babb and Edmund Anable. The three would work from there until a proper chancery could be built.

Leaving the men at 615 Betty Street to attend to Vicariate business, Father Conwell traveled to Seattle to consult doctors about his failing health. It was a lengthy process. In July doctors diagnosed a recurrence of cancer. As a little boy, the bishop had thrown himself on his knees asking for help from Our Lady. This time, he asked the whole Vicariate to respond by throwing itself on its collective knees in public prayer for a cure for Father Conwell. The novenas and prayers began on the feast of St. Ignatius of Loyola, July 30, 1959, and officially ended on the first Friday of August. Unofficially, the bishop hoped everyone would continue praying fervently.

Having deposited <u>The</u> <u>Alaskan</u> <u>Shepherd</u> in the mail the bishop continued assisting at Immaculate Conception in Fairbanks and visiting the missions. Among other concerns he checked on his people in Nenana, and noted the progress at Copper Valley. The school now had all eight spokes of the wheel under roof, and it could accommodate two hundred fifty residents. Materials were on hand for the roofing of the central circle. That central circle was designed as an indoor recreation area for the bitter winter months. In the meantime, one wing of the school contained classrooms on the second floor and a gymnasium on the first.

Watching the progress at Copper Valley brought the bishop satisfaction and hope for the youth of eastern Alaska. Then word came that Father Tom Cunningham died at Barrow of a heart attack on September 3, 1959. His death, a shock for everyone, left the bishop wondering how he could provide spiritual help for peoples of the vast area of far-north Alaska.

Father Tom had been serving in northern Alaska for twenty-five years. His military work brought him renown on the civil level. On the spiritual level he was as widely acclaimed and honored in the Ekimo society. For them he built a church and ministered in fluent Eskimo dialect of the North to the Natives on Little Diomede Island where he brought most of the island's population into the Church.

Farther north at Barrow he was pastor of the Catholic community and cared for the buildings he used for services. His church and residence consisted of two Quonset huts that the Air Force had removed from government property. He had been promised ownership of the huts; however, a deed of ownership had not been delivered to him. When he died he was so important to the military world that <u>Time</u> magazine carried the news. This news report of his death may have given more weight to the bishop's query to the Air Force in October 1959 concerning the matter of the deed of ownership. At any rate, Air Force Colonel James H. Isbell assured Bishop Gleeson that he would do all he could to obtain the deed from the Department of the Navy. Eventually, the deed was obtained and those Quonsets continued in use at Barrow until replaced by the new Saint Patrick parish buildings in the summer of 1992.

After Father Tom's military burial in Fairbanks and other business was completed, the bishop left for his annual Washington attendance at the Bishops' Conference. He took his time on the way back and, because of his mobility, no one contacted him to report that Father Anable had broken his back and could not attend to secretarial duties. Father's accident was an unhappy greeting when Gleeson returned before

Christmas. It would have unfortunate consequences to be dealt with later.

Weary Times: 1960

As with Father Conwell, the years had taken their toll on the bishop's health. He had lost eighty pounds in ten years. Not everyone knew that he no longer traveled with little thought to his safety or comfort or that he now confessed to dreading a trip over highways, especially broken or bumpy highways. Few knew that he had applied to Rome five years before for a coadjutor with right of succession, a request to which Rome had not yet responded. His fears and his health notwithstanding, in January he wrote to Father Fallert, Superior at Copper Valley, asking to be advised as to Brother Hess' jubilee celebration. He wished to arrange his annual schedule of events so that he could include Brother's celebrations.

In January on his way to the retreat and meeting of consultors and priests he made a few visitations, and was in his place ready to begin in February 1960. Present were consultors, the Provincial Superior, Alexander F. McDonald, Bishop Gleeson, and twenty-seven Jesuits from the missions. This was a variation of the 1959 agreement that a retreat was to precede the meeting in alternate years. These meetings, an evolution of the consultor-bishop meetings preceding Bishop

Gleeson's arrival in Alaksa, emphasized a greater collaboration between the Jesuits working in the mission field and the directors of that work, and the retreat lent a spiritual depth to the relationship and planning.

This year the illness of Father Conwell saddened everyone but did nothing to repress the liveliness of the discussion that ranged from education, to politics, and once again to finances. The high cost of transportation continued to be a major concern. Consequently, after the meeting, the bishop began the paperwork required by the civil government for purchasing the boat Matanuska for freighting. In April the government permits arrived, and the Vicariate purchased the Matanuska from surplus for the use of the missions. There are no accounts of its use; however, it was purchased for freighting on the Yukon and according to the financial statements, it belonged to the Church for about a year and cost over $2500 to operate. Again, mission operation of its own freighter was not fiscally as profitable as hoped.

Another visionary project that came to naught was the Pan American Company land the bishop and Father Conwell looked at a few years before. Though its location and size did not exactly suit the need, the land became available at an agreeable price, and the bishop purchased it. A later purchase made the Pan Am piece unnecessary and it was donated as a fund raiser. Some of the speculations bore fruit. For example, from the bishop's office a notice went out on April 21 containing the following information:

On April 15th papers were signed transferring to the Church the ownership of the large house in which the Manager of the F. E. Company lives, and a smaller house just north of the Grade School. A part of this transaction included seven acres of land of which a large square lay directly in front of the elementary school. Occupancy of the houses would not be yielded, necessarily, until the end of 1964. The purchase price was $130,000.00.

News briefs from the bishop's office announced that Father Boileau was to co-chair the Cancer Drive for the Fairbanks area, and the sad word that Alaska Air Line had so far not extended a free or reduced-rate of transport for volunteers working in the Fairbanks area. It is noteworthy that commercial transport used by the priests in Alaska was occasionally reduced in price or donated. Priests working as chaplains for government agencies like the DEW Line and Air Force could ride free on military planes.

Research found no other transactions during the first half of 1960 when on June 13 the bishop fulfilled his commitment to deliver the homily at the blessing and dedication of St. Anthony Church in Anchorage. This second Catholic Church represented an expansion for the new Diocese of Juneau. For Bishop Gleeson on this visit there were no mud streets and no half-built church to remind him of his first visit to Alaska's largest city and his first bank loan as executive of the Catholic Society of Alaska. Anchorage had grown tremendously since 1948.

Upon his return to Fairbanks, Bishop Gleeson granted the men of Immaculate Conception parish permission to organize a Knights of Columbus Council, and then let his thoughts return to news that had reached him on July 12. He found it difficult to think that Father Conwell, his good friend, Chancellor and Secretary for twelve and a half years would not be coming back to Alaska. Father Conwell's death by cancer at the age of forty-seven slowed the bishop perceptibly and put an added strain on his already fragile health.

In the August 16 letter written by the bishop to Father William McIntyre he gives some indication of the burden he carried. He said that he was no longer attempting to attend village conventions, and that he did not press the priests to implement his suggestions for mission activities. His own words give the information more eloquently:

Dear Fr. McIntyre:

The (Eskimo) convention, I suppose, is a thing of history by this time. I hope it went off well this year. I really think it might be developed into something very well worth while for the people and for the Church. Fr. Endal's idea was to make it a meeting point for the villages of the district and to promote the particular village that one happened to belong to. The religious part of the affair was emphasized by Father Fox. I suggested to him one time that part of the program should be to get representatives from the different villages to talk over possibilities of improving conditions, religious and social, in the convention. I don't think he ever saw much value to the suggestion.

Although Bishop Gleeson could have commanded obedience to his ideas; yet, his priests referred to him as a "wait and see" man who pondered a question until it was essential that he answer it then his decision seemed to be written in concrete. Undoubtedly he applied the same philosophy to the missioners work. "Wait and See" whether or not the missioner's ideas are best. Also, he apparently accepted Father Endal's ideas for the convention.

Tired and saddened as he was, the bishop had another unexpected and important decision to make. In September 1960, the twenty-fourth district, in which Father Llorente served as pastor of the church in Alakanuk, sent men to Bishop Gleeson asking if he would allow his priest to serve in the legislature if he were elected. According to Father Llorente, the bishop gave his permission readily because Father O'Connor had lost when he ran for a State Constitutional Convention seat. Llorente thought that the bishop did not perceive the difference in these circumstances; namely, Father Llorente was not officially on the ballot, he did not seek the vote, and the men of his mission initiated the request for permission. All of these points were missing in the former request.

When his village people elected Llorente by a wide margin on a write-in vote, Father said that the bishop, surprised by the win and uncomfortable with the situation, had second thoughts. He directed Father to resign, and to tell his people that he could not serve. Senator Ernest Gruening of Alaska had an official version read into the <u>Congressional</u> <u>Record</u> of January 11, 1961. A small part of Senator Gruening's version reads:

Bishop Gleeson began to have second thoughts—especially in a year when Protestant-Catholic tensions had become an election issue. He asked Representative-elect Llorente to resign, and the priest dutifully sent his Bishop a note of resignation addressed to Alaska's Governor William Egan, together with a letter explaining why it should not be forwarded (If I don't go I failed the voters).

Last week the Eskimos of the 24th district rejoiced when they heard the good news over the short wave. Bishop Gleeson had changed his mind; Father Llorente could serve.

Perhaps the Eskimos were not quite so happy that the bishop had changed his mind when they heard that the area at the mouth of the Yukon was now without a priest. There was no one available to take Father's place on the mission while he represented the people in Juneau. Another unfortunate consequence of the election victory was Bishop of Juneau O'Flanagan's refusal to grant Father Llorente priestly faculties in the Juneau Diocese while he was a member of the legislative body.

During the years of political and social upheaval among the white population of Alaska, priests strove to impart to their Native people the understanding and education needed to survive in that tumultuous, changing environment. Bishop Gleeson lent encouragement, but was careful to advise his priests that they could not operate any commercial undertaking nor could they be an active member of a cooperative. Their involvement could extend only to advice and teaching. The rationale of this policy kept established businesses comfortable and ensured priests the freedom needed to attend to their pastoral duties.

That same policy and rationale applied to government positions. The people Father Llorente represented were happy to have him represent their interests, but now they had to live without a priest in their district. The difficulties due to the shortage of priests were likely to intensify partly because those who served in Alaska were present on a volunteer basis. As the state became more easily reached, its attraction as mission territory decreased.

A Coadjutor Needed

Bernard McMeel's September 24, 1960 article in <u>The Oregon Jesuit</u> gives one an appreciation for the aging bishop's desire for help in his mission activities. The article describes his strenuous travel tasks, especially along the flats bordering the Bering Sea, its bays, sounds, and straits. Father McMeel writes that often the tide was low when the bishop arrived by plane or boat, as it was when he came in the mission boat, The St. Patrick.

That day, he writes, *The tide was so low they had to wait (in the plane) out in the bay until after dark. Then, the Bishop made the trip in through the channel in a kicker boat of Hooper Bay men, who were returning from seal hunting. Jumping from the boat, he slipped on the dock in the dark, broke his ankle, and wrenched his back. He made it to the church with difficulty, helped by two men. Thinking this was a sprained ankle, he confirmed twenty-four, then remained in the village until September 28.* Ready to leave at low tide, *it was necessary for the Bishop to step from one boat to another of several boats, and then to the plane.*

He was flown to Bethel where Father Linssen and Bernard Nevak, his Eskimo pilot and a Chief in Chefornak, had disappeared a few days before. When Bishop Gleeson arrived in the village, the swelling of his leg was so great that he was taken immediately to a doctor. An X-ray showed a broken ankle so the doctor applied a walking cast and, poked around inside whittling away as much material as she dared in an attempt to relieve the pressure caused by the swelling.

The ankle continued to hurt, but the bishop ignored the pain in his attempt to bring spiritual comfort to the exhausted people engaged in the search for the missing men. The body of Bernard Nevak was never recovered, and the seamen grieved for Nevak's people who mourned the loss of their Chief. Eventually, Father Linssen's body was discovered some twenty miles from the boat. From the evidence it was reasoned that the men were overwhelmed in the open sea out of the Kuskokwim River sometime between September 16 and 23.

Father was only forty-one, and the only available priest for the Bethel mission. Father Deschout, hospitalized in Fairbanks when he heard about the accident in Bethel, boarded a plane as soon as he was released from hospital care. He had evangelized many of the people of Bethel, and now, even though he was too crippled to go on a mission journey, he wanted to be there to care for those who came to him.

Having given all the help he could, Bishop Gleeson departed for Fairbanks. By the time he arrived home his cast had collapsed on one side causing a good bit of merriment among the chancery staff. His doctor, too, had difficulty disguising his mirth while he removed the cast. The laughter did relieve some of the sadness everyone felt about the accident. Without that cast the bishop was able to attend, on October 1, a meeting of the newly organized Archbishop Seghers Council of the Knights of Columbus. The men of the Council used the opportunity to bestow on Bishop Gleeson the honors of Third Degree Knight.

The year did not finish on this happy note. The tiny Eskimo community of Sisters, Oblates of Our Lady of the Snows, had been having difficulties for several months. When the bishop returned home from the meeting of the National Conference of Catholic Bishops, he heard that the last three Oblates had left their convent. With a heavy heart, he recognized the dissolution of the community that had lent so much support to the priests and had given children their first sight of an Eskimo Catholic Sister.

Subsequently, two of the former Oblate Sisters continued to feel strongly that they wanted to pursue the religious life, and one of them left Alaska to enter the Ursuline Community. As a member of that Community she earned a Doctorate Degree and returned ten years later to teach at St. Mary's. Another of the young women left with Sisters from another community and soon discovered that their life did not suit her. She returned to the laity. Still, Bishop Gleeson did not officially dissolve the community; thus allowing for a future group to form.

Education: 1961

Except for the school at Holy Cross, all the schools in Alaska were flourishing in 1961. For generations Holy Cross Mission took care of the children boarding at the school and the people living in the village of Holy Cross and its environs. The care extended to hospital care, family counseling, and any other help needed. Now that the faculty consisted of volunteers and the boarders were no longer there, day students and the people of the area were unwilling to help gather firewood and do ordinary clean up and grounds maintenance. While there had always been a shortage of money at the mission, the present problem was exacerbated by the government stipends that made the Native people conscious of income and less willing to be helpful and neighborly. For the most part, they were wholly indifferent to the needs of the mission and its volunteers. Eventually, the school was taken over by the public school system.

Copper Valley School, however, reported an enrollment of a hundred and twenty-six with a waiting list of sixty applicants from many places, even as far away as Africa. Three African students were there on scholarships, and were maintaining honor roll averages. The school at Dillingham had two priests, nine volunteers, and forty-five children. Their difficulty arose from the lack of an experienced administrator and faculty to give it a long-term educational plan.

The difficulties arising from the volunteer program in the school system was felt most by the school at Dillingham. Copper Valley, though new, had an experienced staff to absorb and guide the volunteers. Holy Cross, with its volunteers outnumbering religious overseers, nevertheless, had a long-standing educational program. Dillingham was new and had an inexperienced Principal, a priest or two as experienced instructors and a remaining staff of untrained, poorly oriented volunteers. The bishop, though an experienced teacher and administrator, knew class structure in a significantly different cultural setting. His many Vicariate responsibilities blinded him at times to the problems at places he thought were adequately cared for by those in charge. Dillingham was one of those places.

St. Mary's School was well staffed and had added adult education reading, spelling and arithmetic classes. This was a project dear to the heart of Bishop Gleeson who was confident that the Natives would be poor and vulnerable until they could meet white people on a level of equal education. Since 1955 the students had worked the salmon cannery at St. Mary's with the understanding that the business would be theirs as soon as they learned to manage it. To date the business had prospered and yielded payments of ten thousand-dollars or more each year. This year of 1961 saw some financial and appetite changes. A devaluation of the English pound, a dormant fish market, and young Jews favoring tuna and other fish not favored by their elders caused a sudden drop in earnings from the salmon cannery. The economic impact was a difficult learning situation for the student managers.

Although Monroe High School was not a mission, it was new and it was prospering. Parents, to their long-lasting satisfaction, built an addition to the school for a library and extra classrooms. To further the cause, the bishop donated to the high school the house he had purchased and furnished for the school faculty.

Land for a Chancery

A first step toward a Cathedral Church and Chancery Building was taken with the purchase of a large piece of land on the corner of Airport Way and Peger Road. Though Airport and Peger were nothing but narrow mud lanes, Airport Way did lead to the new airport. This corner property cost a little more than $41,000 and promised to be a prime site in the near future. Excited, Bishop Gleeson called upon Father Spils building skills, and preparation for ground breaking began.

Sobriety asserted itself quickly when the news of Father McElmeel's death at Ketchikan reached Fairbanks on August 16. The veteran Father Joseph McElmeel had been a missionary in Alaska for thirty-seven years. He shepherded the new Vicar Apostolic of Alaska on his first plane ride in 1948, and was a stalwart friend and supporter since his installation. Father McElmeel was known everywhere and represented the link between the founding Fathers of the Alaskan Missions and the missions of the sixties.

Amidst the general sadness, the Church in Fairbanks began preparing for the celebration of Pope John XXIII's eightieth birthday on October 20. The priests, Knights of Columbus, ladies of the Altar Society, Altar Boys, school children and their parents all began laying plans for a joyous celebration. These plans came together and concluded on October 25 with a exultant High Mass and parish party.

The Second Vatican Council: 1962

Early in 1962, Bishop Gleeson devoted his time to everyday affairs and Confirmation trips until the gathering for the annual consultors' meeting. At the meeting the agenda revisited the proposal made some three years previously that mission priests should have a mission plane at their disposal in order to save time and money. Father John Wood, one of the pilots, had been assigned the task of gathering information concerning the proposal.

Father's presentation gave the pros and cons of the trial to the consultors. In short, he found: that a priest-pilot with his own plane could:

- visit his missions more regularly
- spend more time with his people
- have a more elastic schedule
- have Sunday Mass at more than one place
- avoid the inconvenience of cancelled flights.
- make the rounds of his district for approximately $50 compared to the $400 to $600 commercial flight cost.

The greatest **danger** was to the inexperienced pilot. This could be overcome only by many hours of flying. Finally, plane

maintenance could be costly unless the pilots were willing to learn some mechanical skills. In the end, the consultors agreed that airplanes should be made available to the missionaries wherever possible.

After the meeting, priests and bishop returned to the ordinary brisk activities of mission life. Then, in May, excitement surrounded the groundbreaking ceremonies for the Chancery Building. Sidewalk supervisors were just settling into their task at Peger Road and Airport Way when breathtaking news came to the bishop through Egedio Vagnozzi, Apostolic Delegate to the United States. Pope John XXIII had raised The Vicariate of Northern Alaska to the status of a Diocese and named Francis D. Gleeson as the first Bishop of the Diocese of Fairbanks on August 8, 1962. The diocese would remain under the jurisdiction of the Propagation of the Faith in Rome. The announcement would be made public on September 5.

Still recovering from the surprise of the notice, the bishop celebrated fifty years as a member of the Society of Jesus on August 15. With his clergy and laity in attendance, he said a Pontifical Mass in Immaculate Conception Church, followed by a reception and banquet. As reported by the <u>Fairbanks</u> <u>Daily</u> <u>News</u> – <u>Miner</u>, decorations on the large cake at the reception represented the thirty-two residences, churches and schools constructed during his years as Vicar Apostolic of Alaska. Tom

Miklautsch, master of ceremonies, presented him with an album of sixteen sketches. They depicted the various phases of his life. There was also a spiritual bouquet of prayers and good works offered by the people of the Vicariate, and an envelope containing $2500 to pay for his trip to Rome for the Ecumenical Council.

Questioned about the administration of the diocese during his extended absence, he laughed aloud, and answered, *You find out how well they can get along without you.* The "they" referred to Fathers Henry G. Hargreaves, S.J., Vicar General and Chancellor William Babb.

Bishop Gleeson flew to Rome on October 3, 1962. While there he stayed as a guest of the Holy Father at the Hotel Pacific. Asked if he was more awed by the pomp of the Council or his visit to Rome while he was studying in Spain, he responded that he was more impressed by his first visit to the Holy City. He said that being with his peers as a part of the decorous pageantry changed his perspective. Each day as a member of the Second Vatican Council, he listened intently to all the presentations, but found no reason to raise his own voice. In the end, he came away with the impression that the American Bishops were not aggressive enough, perhaps not properly prepared, for all the discussions. He did not say whether he classified himself as too passive or too unprepared.

Reminiscent of his years in Spain, Italian food caused digestive problems for him. His discomfort, however, did not prevent him from attending the meetings. Of all the Council gatherings, he remembered missing only one or two.

ORDINARY OF FAIRBANKS

The single most important happening of 1963 was the installation of The Most Reverend Francis D. Gleeson, D.D., S.J., on February 21 as Bishop of the newly created See of Fairbanks. His Metropolitan, Archbishop Thomas A. Connolly, D.D., presided at the installation which took place at the Immaculate Conception Church. Also present in the sanctuary were Bishop Thomas E. Gill, D.D., of Yakima, who delivered the sermon, and Bishop Joseph P. Dougherty, D.D. There were representatives from several other dioceses, the Society of Jesus, and other religious and lay persons from around Alaska. The choir from Copper Valley School sang for the ceremonies. The reception following the ceremonies rang with exuberant celebration. The Catholic Church in Northern Alaska had come of age.

One of the first tasks addressed by the new diocese was the religious education of Dillingham's Russian Orthodox population. When the Russian Orthodox priest, Father Roshko, arrived in 1955, the religious education of the Russian Orthodox people was left in his hands. The task, however, overwhelmed him. As early as 1958, the Jesuits were considering ways to help Father Roshko. As a preliminary step,

Harold Greif, S.J., gave the consultors a quiet narration during the bishop's celebration of Mass. The narration pointed out the likeness and difference between the Russian Orthodox and Roman Rite liturgy. It was hoped that a concentrated effort could be made during the year to educate the people of the Orthodox belief in the basic tenets of their faith to which they so loyally clung.

Along with increased religious education, the clergy believed that a secure and prideful people would not need alcohol. They hoped to pave the way to security and pride by providing an education that would enable the people to meet their white brothers on an equal footing. Between the adult education effort in the parish and Father William C. Dibb's effort to upgrade the curriculum of the school at Dillingham, expectation ran high that the alcoholic habits of the people could be broken.

Firedrills Should Be Heeded

On March 26 Bishop Gleeson, in Fairbanks, was absorbed in office work when news came by radio that St. Mary's School was on fire. Sister Scholastica, cook at St. Mary's, tells this story:

I was down in the laundry sorting clothes. A boy came with his mattress over his shoulder and he said,

"Sister where will I put this?"

"Well put it where it belongs, on your bed," I said. Then he said,

"But Brother Benish said I should bring it to you."

I said, *"All right. Is there something wrong with that?"*

He said, *"I don't know."*

"All right," I said, *"put it there. I'll take care of it later."* He was barely gone when two more came with their mattresses.

I said, *"Put it there."* Then the fire alarm rang. No, it rang before but we all thought it was a fire drill, so I didn't pay much attention. In those days we didn't. The girls all went out, and one came back and said,

"I need my coat. It is cold out."

She didn't say there was a fire. She just wanted her coat. It was twenty below zero that day, and a sharp wind.

Father Poole passed by with two or three girls. It was sunny out and he wanted to take pictures. He was kind of peeved because the fire alarm did not ring all free yet, and then he came back. He said,

"There is a fire."

So, then, naturally, we went out to see. It was the boys' house. Oh, that wind it was fierce. We were just helpless; we couldn't do anything. They were carrying things out. Brother Benish got everything out of the post office. I don't know how *they did it. Those heavy, heavy safes. They got out what they could. They tried to fight it, but we had very little water. The river was frozen to six feet of ice. Of course, we had the well. The men were pumping, but we couldn't get enough water. We were helpless. The men couldn't get into the place where it started. It was so thick with smoke there. In the end, we had to give up. The root cellar was in that house. All our potatoes and salmon, everything in that house was destroyed not all our food, but everything in the root cellar.*

Well, then our Superior, Mother Margaret Mary, had great devotion to our Blessed Mother, so she took a statue and she put it right there. She took the children to the chapel to pray. She said that she told the Blessed Mother, "That far; no farther."

And do you know, they chopped down the hall to the wall where the statue stood. The flames had already licked that whole wall, when the wind actually shifted clear around and it saved this building.

One of the villagers said, "Why don't you put snow on top of the building?" And so they all made a beeline. The girls cut snow in blocks and the boys relayed the blocks to the roof and piled them on that side as high as they could with snow. When the flames touched it, the water dripped down and put it out.

One Sister, Sister Wivina, she's dead now; she took care of the dinner that day, and she said to me,

"I am not going out. Our Lady will save this building."

Father Poole came by and said,

"Sister, why aren't you out? Within twenty minutes this building will be in flames, too."

She said, "I am not going Father. I am staying here. This building is not going." He shook his head and left.

I said, "Come on Sister. Use your head. Let's go out."

She said, "I am not leaving this place. Our Lady will save it."

When the mail plane came over and saw the flames, the pilot went back to base and brought fire extinguishers for us, but it was too late. The fire was too big.

Gleeson glumly mumbled, *A bad day*, to sum up his emotions as he waited in Fairbanks for information. From the complete destruction of the tiny studio used to teach radio and to broadcast programs into the village homes, investigators determined that a short in the amplifier caused the fire.

Father Poole, as school principal, authorized housing changes for the boys, and school continued despite the odor of baked potatoes and charred salmon. Debris cluttered the landscape and everyone endured dirt, disorder, and lean times. The Air Force men sent tons of potatoes and other vegetables and through the efforts of the Ursuline Sisters some $40,000 was raised. Other generous donors supplied clothing destroyed in the fire. The belongings of the priests were not so easily replaced, especially their library.

Rebuilding was begun, but abruptly discontinued when bulldozers uncovered ice some six feet below the surface. The original building had been erected partially on permafrost ground. Eventually the boys' building rose once more through the efforts of the students.

Copper Valley Dome in Place

The gloom of March lifted somewhat when news arrived from Copper Valley in April that the dome of the central circle was completed. Surrounded by the seven wings of the building, the central area could now be used for dances and sports in severe weather. The next month the school yearbook arrived for the bishop. To his surprise and gratification the students dedicated the Corona Borealis to honor his fifty years as a Jesuit and his fourteen years as Vicar Apostolic of Alaska. With this dedication the students expressed their thanks for the example he projected for them. Secondarily, the Corona also celebrated the year of the Second Ecumenical Council.

Second Session of Vatican Council

To attend the second session of the Vatican Council Bishop Gleeson left Fairbanks on September 23. So convinced was he that his own cooking would solve his digestive problems that he rented an apartment upon his arrival in Rome. However, with that problem solved, he literally walked into another misfortune on December 1. While walking across Cola de Rienzo Square to attend a Council meeting, he was hit by an automobile and suffered severe leg bruises.

It was during this session of the Council that Father Louis Renner received an invitation to meet with Bishop Gleeson. Father was studying Philosophy at the University of Munich when the invitation to visit came. Seminarians and clergy in Europe were cautioned away from the vicinity of Rome during the Council so this invitation was to be treasured as a kindness and because of the consequences of the visit. The latter was in the form of a faculty place in the Language Department of the University of Alaska when Father Renner returned to the United States in 1965. Following Father Renner's placement on the faculty, Father Patrick S. Duffy in Education, Fathers Wallace M. Olson and William J. Loyens, S.J, in Anthropology were accepted on the staff in consecutive years. Though these priests did not wear their cassocks on campus, Bishop Gleeson believed that they wielded a great spiritual influence in the university milieu.

A Year of Surprises

The Jesuit retreat, hosted by Copper Valley in 1964, came to a climax with a Solemn High Mass, at which Father Boileau, Superior of the Missions, was celebrant. Bishop Gleeson presided at the Mass and witnessed the final vows pronounced by Pasquale Spoletini, stationed in Kotzebue, and William C. Dibb, from Holy Rosary Mission School, Dillingham. These promises committed them to the Society of Jesus for life.

The consultors and guest Jesuits had barely returned to their missions when the disastrous earthquake of March 27, 1964 shook Copper Valley to its foundations. William Hunt gives a Richter scale reading as 8.3 and 8.6 and the duration of the shock as a good three minutes. According to his account, the shock was felt over 500,000 miles. In Alaska severe shaking and its attendant damage had been experienced for more than a hundred miles inland. Through the quake, the new state's economic weakness was revealed in a dramatic way when it had to make repairs. Damage in the coastal regions was extensive and repairs extremely costly.

At Copper Valley School no structural damage was done and books and pieces of furniture toppled by the shaking were quickly restored to order. Almost immediately the school was made available as a headquarters for emergency workers and as a shelter for refugees from the gulf coastal region. Though not greatly surprised by the safety of the structure, the bishop was very thankful that it escaped damage.

Surprise Number One

In his capacity as Mission Superior, Father Boileau spent most of his time visiting priests in the bush. On one of his infrequent stops in Fairbanks on April 21, a letter awaited him. Briefly, it read:

To Our beloved son, George Boileau of the Society of Jesus, Titular Bishop-elect of Ausuccoura and likewise appointed Coadjutor to the Episcopal See of Fairbanks with right of succession, greetings and apostolic benediction.

This stunning surprise for Father Boileau came as a great relief for Bishop Gleeson. It also threw the diocese into a frenzy of preparation. A place for the consecration ceremonies became a primary concern. Immaculate Conception Pro-Cathedral in Fairbanks was too small. Sacred Heart Cathedral was not yet constructed, and Cathedrals in the "lower forty-eight" were too far away. When Copper Valley School was suggested, Bishop-elect Boileau quickly agreed saying,

I want to be consecrated among the people I have lived with and with whom I will be associated in the future, and in the land of my fellow missionaries and religious co-workers.

In the midst of these preparations, Bishop Gleeson flew to Rome on July 3 for meetings in preparation for the third session of the Second Vatican Council. He returned to Fairbanks as quickly as possible so that he could be present for Boileau's ordination on July 31, 1964.

His Eminence Francis Cardinal Spellman, Archbishop of New York, assisted by Bishops Gleeson and O'Flanagan, ordained the new Bishop. The celebrations that followed left no doubt as to the appreciation and affection the people of Alaska had for Bishop George Boileau. Little more than a month later, on September 12, Bishops Boileau and Gleeson departed at midnight from the Fairbanks airport to attend the third session of the Second Vatican Council. The session opened on the fourteenth and Bishop Gleeson described the spirit of the Council meetings as one of desire to *update the nonessentials* (of the Church) *without changing essentials.*

As usual meeting schedules left little time for leisure; however, Bishop Gleeson did travel to Florence to visit the Gonzaga University Extension situated in that city. Also, sometime during this third session of the Council, he met the seminarian Angus McDonald. Angus asked to be accepted as a candidate for ordination to the Fairbanks Diocese and, later, arranged for Bishop Gleeson to offer the Holy Sacrifice of the Mass at the High Altar in St. Peters. For this privileged celebration of the Holy Sacrifice the General Superiors of the community of The Little Sisters of Jesus who had their headquarters in Rome attended as representatives of the Sisters serving the Fairbanks Diocese.

Surprise Number Two

At the close of the third session on November 21, the Bishops of Fairbanks returned home where Gleeson found a letter on his desk dated November 23. In it the Apostolic Delegate Egidio Vagnozzi asked for Bishop Gleeson's views on the establishment of a diocese with Anchorage as the See City. He also asked for recommendations regarding the possible boundaries if a See were established. The following are excerpts from the bishop's December 6, 1964 reply:

On my return from Rome to Fairbanks on December 2, your letter of November 23rd was waiting on my desk. The questions raised in it came as quite a surprise and have claimed priority in my thoughts ever since. I can easily agree that Anchorage is at present the most promising development in the new state of Alaska. My immediate reaction to the proposal is that the time is not yet here for such a move.

With regard to the suggested boundaries of the Third Judicial District, I would like to make the following observation:

Both Copper Valley School and Holy Rosary Mission at Dillingham which are now in the Diocese of Fairbanks would belong to Anchorage since both are in the Third Judicial District. Copper Valley School is considerably the largest boarding school we have and was built to replace the antiquated facilities at Holy Cross Mission on the Yukon.

The reasons for the choice of the new location were: first, being nearer to the southern coast, the cost of building would be considerably reduced and also the cost of bringing supplies would be less.

The second reason was: since the Alaska Natives are eventually going to be forced to make their way in white man's civilization, it would be better to have some whites in the school so that the Natives would find out how to live with the changing situation. Most of the present student body at the Copper Valley School come from the interior.

Since the whole set up was intended for Natives and would not be of great value to a Diocese such as Anchorage would likely be, and since the loss of the plant would be a serious loss to the educational effort of the Diocese of Fairbanks, I think that boundaries had better be set that would leave this installation within the jurisdiction of Fairbanks.

The loss of Dillingham would be less of a problem, but, since the whole district and the Aleutian Islands are still decidedly mission territory, I would question the advisability of including it in a new diocese which would not be a mission diocese.

After conferring with Bishop Boileau, later on that same day, the Bishop sent another letter in which he said in part:

In my previous letter on this subject I mentioned a couple of objections to taking the Judicial Division as a boundary description of a new diocese. Bishop Boileau mentioned that he had also made a suggestion of a small modification. I do not know if he mentioned the fact that there is serious question of a change by the State in the Judicial jurisdiction.

With this, both bishops put the matter aside to await further communication.

Loss and Change: 1965

Word of two accidents ushered in 1965. On New Year's Eve, Father William C. Dibb's snowmobile broke down between Marshall and Pilot Station. He had wet feet from standing in water puddled on the ice while he worked on his snowmobile. As a result, he was hospitalized with frostbitten feet. The next day, New Years, William T. McIntyre, left his mission at Alakanuk about noon to travel some ten miles up river where he would say a third Mass for that day at Sheldon Point. Because it was such a short trip he had not taken his usual gear of sleeping bag, snow shovel and other provisions. However, in a short time, he was caught in a whiteout and lost his direction in the windswept, whirling snow. He parked his Ski-doo for the night but could not sleep due to the danger of frostbite. The next day he had not gone far before he noticed a considerable amount of water on the ice. Fearful that he was going in the wrong direction he stopped and did what he could to build shelter from the sharp wind and freezing rain that had closed in. Rescued three days later, he was rushed to the hospital where expert treatment of his lungs and frostbitten limbs saved his life. Another casualty of the bitter weather was

Father Roshko in Dillingham. He had taken a nine months leave in 1962/63, and gave up and left Alaska in January 1965.

Some of the anxiety generated by the two accidents was softened a few days later by an enthusiastic letter from Father Poole in Portland. In his letter he delineated his prospects for collecting enough money to erect and maintain a radio station in Nome. He reported that by January 9, 1965 he had banked $2000 toward an estimated $64,000 project. It was the kind of enthusiastic foresight Bishop Gleeson appreciated, and just the thought of Poole's displayed initiative added to the joy of Gleeson's seventieth birthday on January 28. An autographed blessing from Pope Paul VI was the real icing on Bishop Gleeson's birthday cake.

Unfortunately, the bishop would soon need the strength afforded by that blessing when he heard on February 25 that Bishop Boileau had died at Riverton, Washington. There had been no warning before Bishop Boileau's fatal heart attack. Because Boileau was known and loved by a great many in Alaska shock gripped the entire Fairbank's community and radiated into the villages of Alaska. A drawn and haggard looking Gleeson delivered the eulogy during the Pontifical Mass of Requiem offered at the Cathedral of St. James in Seattle on March 2, 1965. In part he said:

To my mind there was one predominant feature and a ruling spirit—the spirit of an Apostle of Jesus Christ. All the Apostles of history have differed from each other. They fitted their age and the circumstances in which they lived. All of them, however, had one trait in common—that was their enthusiastic love and complete dedication to Jesus Christ, the Son of God. This love and this dedication inspired in them a willingness, a burning zeal to undertake any labor, no matter how hard, any suffering, no matter what the cost.

In The Alaskan Shepherd, Catherine Calvin described Bishop Boileau as *endowed with above average intelligence, combined with a most charming and friendly personality.* He was buried in Fairbanks in the land that he loved, amid the people with whom he lived and worked. The students of Monroe High School mourned his passing, remembered his love and concern for them, and memorialized him in the student yearbook. Monroe's full size gymnasium/assembly hall bears his name.

With Bishop Boileau's death, Bishop Francis Gleeson had once more to demonstrate his willingness to accept the unacceptable. Deeply disappointed he again bent to the task of single handedly shouldering the weight of the diocese. The next month, on April 24, he conducted one of his happier duties when he ordained to the priesthood Angus McDonald at the Pro-Cathedral of the Immaculate Conception. Father

McDonald was the first priest ordained in the new diocese. He was also the first secular priest ordained for the diocese. Though he did not serve in the Fairbanks Diocese all the time, he never lost his admiration for Bishop Gleeson.

Just over a month later, in June 1965, the bishop plunged into a major building project. Ground breaking for the cathedral was discontinued three years earlier because of an appeal by Father Francis McGuigan, S.J., who was in charge of the Fairbanks Catholic School system. Father pleaded,

I approached him (Gleeson) and told him that our gym was completely inadequate, and asked that instead of putting any more money into other building projects at that time, if he would, please, grant us the privilege of building a new gymnasium. Which he did.

As usual, the bishop was in dire need of money. While Father McGuigan was building the Monroe High School gymnasium, Bishop Gleeson was benefiting from his charitable period of waiting. An expansion project prompted the City Fathers to approach him and ask for a piece of the acreage he had purchased as a cathedral site. In order to widen and pave Airport Way, they asked to purchase a strip of land bordering Airport Way. Their offer was half again as much as he had paid for the whole parcel. The transaction allowed the bishop to recover the price of his cathedral land and to begin building the church.

When the diocese began construction in earnest in June of 1965, several seminarians came up from Washington and work progressed quickly. The structure was enclosed before winter allowing interior work to continue into the spring. On April 3, 1966, Palm Sunday, one year after structural work began Sacred Heart Cathedral opened its doors for limited service. It was not dedicated until June 17, 1966. Built at a time when the Church was emphasizing simplicity and de-emphasizing architectural beauty, the building stands as a symbol of its time in history.

Another kind of building was also going foreword in the diocese. Inspired by the directives of Vatican Council II, active involvement in Church affairs moved forward in virtually all denominations. Church groups were mingling beyond their single Church entity. For the first time people were learning something of the beliefs of their neighbors and even seeing the inside of churches outside their own belief. Bridges of knowledge and understanding were being built.

In his teaching capacity Bishop Gleeson released a Directive on Ecumenism during Advent of 1965, which laid out the basic tenets a Catholic must keep in mind while seeking closer communion with peoples of other faiths. Among them was his caution, *One cannot both be and not be what one professes to be.* He impressed upon Alaskan clergymen in the van of the movement to make haste slowly. While it was not his intent to impede progress, he did most certainly advocate thorough understanding. Nevertheless, it was this kind of prudent directive that now won for Bishop Gleeson among some of his clergy the reputation of fearful, old and hesitant.

Those days in Alaska saw numerous non-denominational meetings that explored Church and social problems and their impact on the Native people. Though many problems were identified, no denomination offered wholly acceptable solutions.

Ecumenism and Social Issues

This "old and fearful" bishop actively attended many of the joint meetings of the Churchmen. One of those meetings was held at Copper Valley School. While there the bishop arranged to meet privately with Paul J. Dixon, a politically knowledgeable and socially interested Catholic layman. Subsequent talks led to a way for Bishop Gleeson to step around the hurdles raised for priestly involvement in social issues. In an experimental move toward expediting Church involvement in social issues he engaged Mr. Dixon on March 31, 1966.

Dixon was to educate, organize, and guide the people of St. Marys and neighboring villages in the steps toward becoming a recognized political entity within the United States and Alaska governmental structure. Only with the full consent and desire of the Alaskan villagers could Mr. Dixon hope to succeed in attaining the bishop's goal that would enable the Natives of the area to become substantial, independent citizens eligible for government benefits. Before long, Dixon's tutelage brought several villages to tribal strength even where they had not attained political standing. As part of this effort he organized twenty-four mission villages into a group that took the name Hillcrest, Inc.

Most notably, he guided St. Marys to the status of a second class city at which point the bishop signed over to the Village Council all the land (about forty-five square miles) not required for the use of the school. The cannery business would also become theirs when they had acquired enough knowledge to manage the business.

Early in July of 1966 the bishop suggested to the Village Council a plan of Management by a Board of Directors and a plan of Profit Sharing with the village and individual workers and fishermen. The plan was presented in writing to the Village Council on September 21, 1966 and accepted at once for the organization of the Yukon Packers. A short time later Mr. Roger B. Buchanan, Field Examiner for the NLRB, received a document from Father Rene Astruc, S.J., showing the Yukon

Packers as operated by a religious organ, its owner a Corp. Sole and its purpose to educate Native people in modern business methods. The revenues would offset the cost of the local Mission School.

In 1967, Father Paul B. Mueller, S.J., designated the St. Marys area the most impoverished in the whole of the United States. Dixon's efforts enabled them to obtain a grant and loans amounting to $426,000 for an ocean-going boat dock, a cold storage facility for their salmon fishermen and the canning business, and a road and community center to accommodate travelers using their airport. St. Marys grew into a first class city operating its own school system.

A Coach Is Honored

In the fall of 1965, as a surprise for his old friend, John Heinrick, the bishop traveled to Tacoma for a "John Heinrick Night" at Bellarmine to honor its initial and longtime football coach. As a young man Mr. Gleeson had tried to use Heinrick's coaching methods in his teaching. Later he learned to modify the methods, but he always maintained the highest respect and admiration for the coach. Other guests attest that it was a warm and touching meeting for both men. In a thank you letter to the bishop, Heinrick expressed his amazement: *I could not believe my eyes when you walked into the banquet hall.*

Emotionally, 1965 had run the gamut from great happiness to deep sorrow and back to happiness, a roller coaster difficult for anyone of any age, especially so for Bishop Gleeson at seventy-one. He perceived travel as a drain on his physical reserves. He yearned for a Coadjutor.

Even though he acknowledged that change became harder as one grew older, he impressed on his priests and people the necessity of implementing the changes recommended by Vatican Council II and actively encouraged his people to study and embrace them. He explained the Council documents and the reasoning that produced them whenever the opportunity presented itself. Involved as he was in making the documents a part of everyone's life, he was not too surprised when he received a message from the Papal Delagate. Reading the message, though, was like receiving an electrical jolt.

More Major Changes

His Holiness, Pope Paul VI, apprised Bishop Gleeson of a change in administrative structure through a letter from Apostolic Delegate Vagnozzi, on February 2, 1966. As he read, the bishop was in turn surprised, saddened and disappointed by the following message:

It is my pleasure to inform you that His Holiness, Pope Paul VI, has established a new archdiocese with the title of <u>Anchorage</u>. *Monsignor Joseph T. Ryan has been named the first archbishop. The announcement will be made public on Wednesday, February 9.*

Alaska's newspaper coverage after the announcement quotes the bishop as saying, *Neither Bishop O'Flanagan nor I were aware that the creation of an archdiocese was imminent.* Neither bishop had received any communication concerning the proposed archdiocese since December 1964. What was probably an even greater surprise to Bishop Gleeson was the inclusion of Copper Valley School and Holy Rosary, Dillingham, within the archdiocesan boundaries. For this he blamed himself for not being more assertive in his advice concerning boundary lines even though he had made very clear recommendations. Again, the missionary work was in the hands of God.

Bishop O'Flanagan's diocese fared far worse than Fairbanks when it lost Anchorage its only large population center and possible place for growth. At the banquet following the installation ceremonies for Archbishop Ryan, Bishop O'Flanagan toasted the new archbishop with, *As a mark of my esteem I give you Anchorage.* Bishop Gleeson, it is said, followed this with, *I do give into your care one of the Aleutian Islands, and better than that, I give you my heart in Copper Valley.* It brought down the house. While the audience was rising and clapping, those near Bishop Gleeson noticed that he was white and seemed near fainting.

Both the Juneau and Fairbanks diocese were attached to the Archdiocese of Anchorage with Fairbanks continuing under the protection of the Propagation of the Faith in Rome. Subsequently, as both Bishops Gleeson and Boileau had indicated in their statement about the boundaries for the proposed archdiocese, Anchorage was not prepared to support mission territory. The first to fall victim was the Mission of the Holy Rosary at Dillingham. It closed in May 1966.

During that summer work on the cathedral in Fairbanks progressed and the bishop continued the normal work of his missionary diocese. At a meeting in Anchorage, he met with Paul Dixon and engaged his services as procurator for the Diocese of Fairbanks. Toward the end of summer on August 20 he gave Father Fox permission to send Native women who persisted in their desire for the religious life to Wichita, Kansas for religious training.

A Quiet Statement

With Native women entering religious life Bishop Gleeson realized, as did many of the Jesuits, that the Native laity had much to give to the Church if the priests could find a way to tap into their talents. The opportunity came at the autumn meeting of the United States Bishops Conference where Gleeson made one of his rare statements.

The conference had a long agenda of Vatican Council recommendations to consider with the limelight on such matters as Liturgy and Ecumenism. Subjects considered of less urgency were to be relegated to another time. When consideration of the Permanent Diaconate was about to be tabled, Archbishop Francis T. Hurley of Anchorage said,

Almost apologetically Gleeson stated that he felt no special competence on the subject of the Permanent Diaconate. He noted simply that Vatican Council II had authorized its restoration, and that for him in the vast mission fields of Alaska this meant the possibility of an official representation of the Church in remote areas.

In response the bishops began a discussion of the recommendation with the result that several dioceses inauguated a Permanent Diaconate Program.

When the bishop returned to Alaska, he celebrated the holidays on cathedral land in temporary quarters near his nearly completed Cathedral Church.

An Exhausted Bishop

On January 18, 1967, Bishop Gleeson wrote to John J. Kelley, Jesuit Provincial of the Oregon Province:

Yesterday I crossed the seventy-two mark and it helped to convince me that it is about time to make some provisions for a successor. Accordingly, I have written to the Delegate asking him to get the machinery moving. I have also notified Propaganda Fide in Rome of my wishes in the matter so I suppose you will be hearing something officially before long. I thought it would be well for you to know in advance that this action has been taken.

Whether Bishop Gleeson had begun to cut back on his mission travels is difficult to ascertain. With St. Mary's just upriver from Mt. Village, the bishop may have visited with Father Fox at the school. However, there is an interesting April 16 bulletin from Father Fox in which he says that the bishop had sixty-two to Confirm on his recent visit because he had not been to Mountain Village for thirteen years.

The village had outgrown the church building, so there were two Masses on days of obligation and twenty-five to thirty people at daily Mass. This population growth was true in most Native villages since medical attention had eliminated tuberculosis, and instructions in personal hygiene and health care cut infant mortality to a minimum and extended life expectancy. Medical attention accounted for a noticeable growth in the number of Catholics in the Diocese of Fairbanks, too. Growing population also highlighted the truth of the bishop's assertion that building would have to begin again as soon as most of the original needs were fulfilled. His remark could also have meant that the ravages of time would make rebuilding a necessity.

Attending a plenary session of the National Council of Catholic Bishops from April 10-13, Bishop Gleeson reported on the Permanent Diaconate in the United States citing its usefulness in home mission territory; namely; the South, the Southwest, and Alaska. Afterward, he returned home to host the visiting Father General of the Jesuits, Pedro Arrupe. Many took particular note of Father Arrupe's special trip to the once proud mission of Holy Cross. Later, when he by-passed Copper Valley School, which no longer belonged to the Jesuit mission territory, the sadness of those with the visitor and of those who noted his passage was palpable. The Catholic community acknowledged the presence of the Jesuit Father General in Fairbanks by filling the new, not quite finished, Sacred Heart Cathedral to capacity when he concelebrated on April 24, 1967.

Because the cathedral was close to completion, the bishop had put the Eighth Avenue house up for sale to help finance his chancery. In place of the house he and his staff lived in a temporary wooden building erected near the Cathedral Church and the Father General had the opportunity to stay in it while visiting. For approximately two years, it served as home and offices for Bishop Gleeson, his chancellor and secretary. Afterward, it became home to volunteers and then a House of Prayer.

A permanent chancery and living quarters for Gleeson and his staff was just barely begun when the flood of 1967 filled the excavation for the chancery and halted the work for the remainder of the year. From August 14 to 21, 1967, flood waters claimed the whole of the Tanana River basin to nine feet above flood tide. Fairbanks city's centennial preparations were demolished, and Immaculate Conception Church basement with its meeting hall and priests office quarters, Monroe High School's new gymnasium, and more than a foot of the first floor of the Sisters' house were inundated. Watermarks remained on the convent walls for at least two decades, and much of the gymnasium floor had to be replaced.

Newspaper photographs show the bishop with a shovel helping in the cleanup around the church. Piling misfortune upon misfortune for the bishop a group of people saw this as an opportunity to close the schools. To some of these, he said,

I'm going to have a Catholic High School here if I have to teach in it myself. Others were simply told, *School will open on time.*

Flood damage was still being repaired in the city when, on October 26, the <u>Anchorage</u> <u>Daily</u> <u>News</u> "Letters to the Editor" carried an explanation from the Sisters of Charity for their July 1, 1968 projected closure of St. Joseph Hospital in Fairbanks. Because this was the city's only hospital, blame fell on the bishop for not stepping in to prevent the closing of the facility. Some of those bitter comments came from critical Jesuits even though it was a matter wholly within the jurisdiction of the Sisters of Providence. In reality a city hospital opened about the same time that Sisters Hospital closed. It is possible that the Sisters withdrew because of the projected city hospital.

Misfortune must cease at some point and word from St. Mary's School was that turning point. In August word from the Yukon Packer venture showed the salmon selling at a good price. Sadly, when the cannery became a Native owned business, the people were unable to maintain it. Some Fathers blamed the demise on the inability of the Native owners. That is a questionable position. The venture was stabilized and the new owners were thoroughly acquainted with procedures and administration. Changing times more likely caused the closing. At any rate, the equipment was slowly sold off.

The Church in Alaska was aware of the social changes in the mission villages; nevertheless, everyone, in and out of the Church milieu, was taken by surprise at the rapidity with which changes occurred. In response the Church established a Socio-Economic Advisory Committee.

So many misfortunes coming in one year made nineteen hundred sixty-seven a particularly difficult year; therefore, the bishop received the Papal announcement, dated December 6, with glad relief. The subject of the announcement was the appointment of *the Reverend Robert L. Whelan, S.J., as Titular Bishop of Sicilibia and Coadjutor with the right of succession to Your Excellency.* He could now rest easier knowing that the Church would have a Bishop if he should die suddenly.

A Coadjutor Is Consecrated

The ordination of Father Robert L. Whelan took place on February 22, 1968, at Sacred Heart Cathedral. Apostolic Delegate Archbishop Luigi Raimondi presided with Archbishop Joseph T Ryan as Co-consecrator. Almost immediately, Bishop Whelan began ministering among the 14,504 Roman Catholics in this 409,849 square mile missionary diocese. The two bishops worked together on the usual diocesan business. In addition Bishop Gleeson shared his Council experiences whenever asked to do so. At an ecumenical meeting in Fairbanks on January 27, 1968, he spoke of his insights on the work of Vatican Council II, especially as it pertained to ecumenism. However, he considered the <u>Freedom of Conscience</u> pronouncement the most progressive of the Council pronouncements.

Implementing a Council directive, he invited the priests to a Senate Formation Meeting to be held on February 19. Among the subjects discussed was the instruction to turn the altar so that the priest stood facing the people, and, of course, the use of English for the liturgy. Father Fox later wrote that the children paid more attention at Mass after the altar was turned around. He also commented that a hundred of his young people were attending the government run schools and that most did not keep in touch with the village. He did not comment on their religious commitments.

The Chancery Building Rises

With the onset of spring weather several Jesuit Brothers came up from Portland. They drained the excavation made for the chancery building before the flood of 1967, put in the foundations, and raised the wall during the summer. Interior work was completed during the winter months and the long awaited Chancery opened in July of 1968.

Once again the bishop divided his attention between Fairbanks and St. Marys. He watched with interest as the people of St. Marys continued their drive to gain control over their lives through education. These people, it must be remembered, had migrated with their children from Akulurak at the mouth of the Yukon when the St. Mary's boarding school moved upriver to the Andreafski site. Their life had changed from hunter-fisherman-gatherer to a more village style with fishing as the chief industry. They were benefiting too from government loans and education in health issues. Now oil would cause even more changes. The Natives had practically no money for speculation so the land auction could not profit them.

However, state activities benefited all citizens as the exploration for oil in Alaska brought high revenues. To make it possible for the citizenry to benefit a kind of silent auction was organized whereby a citizen could write a check for a piece of land at a small price per acre and register that check along with another small amount for the bid. The bids were then put on a blind drawing and the winner would possess the acreage at a very small price.

Oil speculators who saw specific plots as possible sites for exploration often approached the lucky new owners making high offers, and sellers sometimes became instant millionaires.

Among those bidding were some of the priests and Bishop Gleeson. The bishop often won on his lottery bids and several of his winnings were looked upon as likely oil sites. When he sold his lottery winnings, the Church in Alaska also became a winner.

Although the bishop continued visiting missions, he was tired. On July 18, approaching the Council's mandatory retirement age of seventy-five, he wrote to Rome asking that his retirement be expedited as soon as possible. Within weeks he received word that his petition had been accepted and was to go into effect at once. Bishop Robert Whelan succeeded him as Bishop of Fairbanks on November 30, 1968 and was formally installed on February 13, 1969, just twenty-seven days after Gleeson's seventy-fifth birthday.

RETIREMENT: 1969-1983

Retirement for Gleeson meant handing on responsibility for the Diocese to a younger and stronger man. After retiring Bishop Gleeson did not infringe on Bishop Whalen's authority in any way. Retirement to him meant that he could serve Alaska in other ways; that is, by returning to classroom teaching, by obeying the current bishop and Jesuit directives, by serving local needs. According to Jesuit rules, he could live anywhere he chose. He chose Alaska because he believed he could be of service to its people.

Since his days at Bellarmine High School, he had loved teaching young people and felt that this was his primary talent. With Monroe High School just across town, he applied for a teaching position and was welcomed to the faculty as instructor for afternoon Spanish classes. To his dismay, he soon realized that he had underestimated the temper of the times and the diversity of ambition and ability present in modern youth. He had before him a liberal mix of students, many with little background in study habits and language preparation. Some were prepared for study, but lacked ambition and interest. Another group was ready to accept his teaching and profit from it. Unlike the highly motivated, well disciplined, ambitious young men of seminary classes these youths lived in a worldly atmosphere of skepticism and personal freedom that fed on challenging authority.

In less than two years, he decided that his energies might better be spent in other pursuits and resigned from Monroe's faculty in June. During the summer of 1971, he devised another schedule. He walked three miles to the home of the Little Sisters of Jesus to say Mass for them. He did grocery shopping and, on occasion, cooked for the Jesuit community, studied the Greek and Latin commentaries of the Church, kept up with correspondence, and prayed, always prayed. Visitors to his room often found him sitting in his rocker meditating on the rosary. Evenings he sometimes shared a meal at the home of a friend or family. More often, he was at home with his Jesuit community. After the evening meal, he watched the news, enjoyed good conversation and a hand of pinochle.

Many stories revolve around dinners at the home of friends. Once, it is said, Mrs. Stepovich telephoned to express concern because she had been told he was not well enough to attend her dinner. Immediately, he answered, *Who said?* Another time, while playing pinochle at the Harkovich home, Mrs. Harkovich was partnering with the bishop. Her husband complained that she was overbidding her hand. Chuckling softly, Gleeson came back, *Well, you know, John, you've got to know what to do with them when you've got them.* He continued to visit with the Sisters staffing the Fairbanks Catholic schools, and after dinner enjoyed playing pinochle with them and their visitors.

In his later years, he had hearing difficulties when he was in a group. In fact, it was at a Christmas party for the volunteers given by the Sisters in the "White House" that he mentioned his problem. He was sitting next to the tree, smiling at the antics of the guests. One of the Sisters slipped into a neighboring chair and attempted to draw him into conversation. Quickly he cupped his ear to shield it from extraneous noise.

He always attended these parties as well as other functions in deference to his friends or the people of the diocese. For himself, he delighted in cooking and serving a dinner to a group he had invited for the occasion. Especially during the holidays, he enjoyed preparing a meal for the religious of the diocese. One bright and beautiful day near Christmas he was working in the kitchen when Sister Angela who worked on the diocesan staff, came in singing with abandon. When she saw the bishop, she stopped short and said, *It's beautiful, isn't it?* Immediately, Gleeson responded, *What? The singing?* Sister replied in his own language, *Hmmm.*

There is a tendency to believe that once a person retires there is no more connection with the former occupation. For Bishop Gleeson that was not so. He was still a Bishop and, as such, continued to be interested in all things related to the Church. He attended meetings when it was possible, read pertinent materials to keep abreast of Church business, visited with and addressed groups when he was invited, and continued to be present to anyone who came to him. Once, when he was traveling with Bishop Whelan, the pilot of their small plane told Bishop Whelan to let the old man board first. Without cracking a smile, Gleeson said, *You mean, let the older gentleman board first, don't you?*

Most of his years continued to be highlighted by outstanding circumstances. The first of these came on February 4, 1969 when he received an official communication from the Apostolic Delegate to the United States, Cardinal Raimondi, containing his appointment as Titular Bishop of Cuicul in Numidia. This new diocese was a normal transfer attendant upon retirement. However, with this documentation was a wholly unexpected title of dignity. A medallion of the Papal Arms, to be worn over the pectoral cross, proclaimed him a Bishop Assistant at the Papal Throne.

The Pope had empowered him to impart the Apostolic Benediction with the Plenary Indulgence once a year. Also, there was a place reserved for him as a Papal Assistant in Papal chapels, and gave him precedence over other prelates of his rank and order if summoned when the Eucharistic Sacrifice was concelebrated with the Roman Pontiff.

The honor had a special significance because it was granted out of the usually scheduled time for such largess, and well before he had served twenty-five years as bishop which was the usual time frame for such an honor. Though he cherished the thoughtfulness of the Papal gift, the closing line of the communication, *This dignity attaches you more closely to the See of Peter,* meant more to this quiet man than the trappings of office.

When he was studying for ordination in Spain, young Francis had not passed the test for the fourth course. By itself the scholastic failure meant little, the real heartbreak for Francis was the tradition that indicated he would not be allowed to take the fourth vow that bound the Jesuit to Papal service. Since Vatican Council II, Bishop Gleeson had requested permission to take this vow and was told that his position as bishop made such a vow unnecessary; hence, the Papal words, *This dignity attaches you more closely to the See of Peter* were precious to him.

His joy was overshadowed by the heart-wrenching knowledge that Copper Valley School would close in June of

1971. There was no comfort in his having recognized the decision as inevitable when the Archdiocese of Anchorage was erected with its ill-advised boundary lines. Even though there is every indication that Bishop Gleeson had presented a strong case for keeping the school within mission territory, he assumed the blame for Dillingham and Copper Valley missions being placed within urban boundaries. Some of the Jesuits made it clear that *they* also blamed him.

Taking a broad view a number of the Copper Valley graduates and their former teachers looked upon the closure as inescapable. They pointed out that boarding schools were declining in popularity as the state public school system opened facilities in even the smallest communities. They also took other considerations into account, such as, the temper of the times, and the changing economic climate. The group most affected by the closure were the Canadian Indians who had migrated into the area. Father Buchanan had first planned the school for them, and they were furious at its closing. First vandalized and then gutted by fire the once beautiful building lay for many years as a forlorn scar on the valley floor.

A month after Copper Valley School closed in eastern Alaska, a new strong radio signal went out from Nome in western Alaska. Listeners on July 14, 1971 might not have recognized it as a Gleeson legacy; nevertheless, it was Bishop

Gleeson who gave permission and paved the way for the station. It is true that Father Poole kept his wish before the bishop by channeling radio broadcasts from a St. Mary's school studio into village homes, drawing attention to a money raising effort, and amassing reasons for establishing a broadcasting station.

To the consternation of Father Paul B. Mueller, S.J., the pastor of Nome in 1966, Bishop Gleeson removed him and assigned Father Poole as pastor with permission to build a radio station. Immediately, Father began organizing construction for his long-held dream. When KNOM went on the air on July 14, 1971, letters of blessing and congratulations poured into Nome from around the world, from the Papal Palace to the Presidential White House in Washington and all the social levels in between. From his Washington White House President Nixon described the station as *Alaska's new education-oriented radio station*.

A year and a half after the KNOM debut the results of a research project by the University of Alaska were published. The study identified the effects of different high schools on the mental health, achievement, and identity formation of Eskimo and Indian adolescents. To the great joy of Bishop Gleeson and all those involved in the education of the Native children, Dr.

Judith Kleinfeld's paper, published on June 12, 1973, concluded:

The boarding schools begun by Bishop Francis D. Gleeson are by far the most successful schools in Alaska for Indian and Eskimo students. The students graduating from the Catholic boarding schools tend to be strong people who are at ease in the world. Students from St. Mary's and Copper Valley tend to be the most successful at the university. And they are more likely to become useful adults in their home villages.

Bishop Gleeson was still relishing Kleinfeld's accolade when, on June 17, the Fairbanks community celebrated his Silver Jubilee as Bishop. Actually the community was honoring two effective bishops, their retired Bishop Gleeson and Archbishop Charles John Seghers. The latter's celebration was a Centenary festivity throughout Alaska for the Archbishop who planted the seeds of faith and consecrated Alaska's soil with his blood.

For Bishop Gleeson's anniversary, Rome granted a Papal Blessing and to complete his observance he traveled to his hometown, Yakima. While there he attended on October 18 the ordination and installation of Nicolas E. Walsh, D.D. The new bishop later wrote to thank him for his presence and his support, and Gleeson relived the joys of his own ordination in 1973.

The following year the students of St. Mary's School on the Andreafski produced a booklet that gave an historical background for the school and St. Marys City. In it they thanked the bishop for his part in establishing the incorporated city under Native governance with no religious involvement. The students also included a thank you for the 133.23 acres of Church land that Bishop Gleeson deeded to the city. The phrase "with no religious involvement" had a special significance that was not lost upon the bishop. He appreciated the special gratitude shown for his gift of freedom to them when he overrode the advice of Jesuit consultors who considered developing St. Marys as a model village under religious rule.

The next year, 1975, Bishop Gleeson had the satisfaction of knowing that Native Deacons were taking their place in the Roman liturgy. The first Eskimo was ordained to the diaconate on February 8. This was tangible evidence that his diffident words at the Bishops' meeting of 1966 had made a difference.

There were many cherished memories of events, celebrations and awards. All, except for the honor Bishops Assistant to the Papal Throne, were overshadowed by the Saint Robert Bellarmine Award presented to him at the 1977 graduation ceremonies at Bellarmine Preparatory School. This, the school's highest award, he treasured along with his Papal honors.

BELLARMINE PREPARATORY SCHOOL

Proudly Bestows Upon

Bishop Francis D. Gleeson, S.J.

For 49 Years of Inspirational Leadership in Education

this eleventh

St. Robert Bellarmine Award

This award is presented to Bishop Francis D. Gleeson, S.J., for his pioneer work as a teacher and rector at Bellarmine from 1928-1939. It also honors his untiring zeal on the missions in Alaska where, inspired with a strong sense of the presence of the Holy Spirit and with a realization that his efforts were solely for the greater glory of God, he begged and borrowed money and built a mission school system throughtout Alaska. The University of Alaska now reports "the Catholic boarding schools are by far the most successful schools in Alaska for Indian and Eskimo students."

Well has he lived out the motto on his coat of arms, <u>Adveniat Regnum Tuum,</u> helping bring about the kindly presence of Christ.

Bellarmine Preparatory School salutes you, Bishop Francis Gleeson.

Daniel C. Weber, S.J.

President

June 1977 A.M.D.G.

For a while thereafter, life seemed to attain some quietude until, on June 21, 1980, a heart-stopping bulletin from Bishop Whalen's office came to the people of Fairbanks and the missions. The bulletin read: *I am sorry to have to inform you that Bishop Gleeson suffered an accident in which he broke his hip.* Later word revealed that the bishop was among a group of priests who drove to Anchorage for the jubilee of Father Vincent P. Kelliher, S.J. From Anchorage the group took the ferry to Valdez and continued by car to Fairbanks (335 miles). At Paxson Lodge, about half way, they stopped for rest. Ascending the lodge steps, Gleeson overbalanced on the slightly higher top step, fell backward and broke his hip. With help, he re-entered the car and rode to Fairbanks before going to a doctor. After surgery, his hip healed well and he returned to the Jesuit residence on July 12, 1980.

Evidence of his complete healing was his presence in the receiving line in Anchorage to greet Pope John Paul II on February 26, 1981. According to Bishop Michael H. Kenny of Juneau, he welcomed the Pope *in the manner of a proud host welcoming a visitor to his domain.*

Later that same year, Gleeson took a six-week tour through western United States to visit relatives and friends. He was then eighty-six years of age. When, in 1982, he celebrated seventy years as a Jesuit, he divested himself of all his savings.

The major portion of the money, ten thousand dollars, he gave to establish the Monroe Foundation, a scholarship fund for deserving students.

On occasion, Bishop Gleeson celebrated Mass in the Cathedral. One winter day, when Bishops Gleeson, Whelan and the priests were preparing to give the blessing at the end of Mass, Gleeson suddenly disappeared behind the altar. By the time people realized that he had fallen, his head appeared and he quipped, *So do the leaders fall.*

Over the years the Harkovich family and the bishop became good friends so it was not unusual for the family to invite him to their home for dinner on his eighty-eighth birthday. During the meal their three-year-old son asked, *How old are you?* Upon being told, the boy responded, *You're lucky. Most people are dead by that age.* Everyone, especially the bishop, greeted his candor with laughter.

Because the bishop was not one to complain, his brother priests worried a bit when he confessed that he was not feeling well. His discomfort persisting, he decided in April to consult his doctor, James Lundquist, who checked him into Fairbanks Memorial Hospital where he was given a thorough examination. When asked about the bishop's last days, Dr. Lundquist spoke in a tone of wonder and sadness. *He was recovering, getting stronger, and was almost ready to go home, although he had expressed to several that he was ready to die.* The nurses affirmed his growing strength and loved him as an extraordinarily good patient who could be depended upon for a witty remark to lighten a heavy day.

Bishops Whelan and Gleeson had a long visit the night before Bishop Gleeson died. And during part of that conversation, Gleeson said that when he first applied to enter the Society of Jesus he was turned down because of his health.

The nurses on the morning of April 30, 1983 reported that he rose by himself about 5:30, visited with those on duty, sat in his chair for a while, washed up, and taking his rosary, he went back to bed. There, he settled himself and, holding the rosary crossed his hands on his chest and went to sleep for the last time. *It was almost,* in Lundquist's words, *as though he had made up his mind that this was the time to die, as though he willed it. Like, 'Father, I'm coming.'* The image is reminiscent of the time he and his sister, Anna, decided they had had enough of camping and walked home.

While writing these final pages, thoughts of an evening visit on April 29 often surface. He was vigorous and interested enough in world affairs to ask for a <u>Time</u> and <u>Newsweek</u> magazine if they were available. A half-hour later he was sitting in bed, waiting. While opening <u>Time</u> he said a polite, *Thank you* and a dismissive, *You can go home now.* According to the hospital staff, no visitor conversed with him after that.

May He Rest in Peace

Clergy of all ranks, including the recently ordained Eskimo Deacons, his sister Anna and as many friends as could make the journey paid their respects to Bishop Gleeson. Sacred Heart Cathedral was filled for the Pontifical Mass of Requiem for the last Vicar Apostolic of all of Alaska, and the first Bishop of the Fairbanks Diocese. During the homily Bishop Robert Whelan reminded those present that Bishop Gleeson was patiently waiting for the angels to announce his death knowing that he would rise again to be with Christ. Not to be left out, the Holy Father sent a telegram that Bishop Whelan read,

The Holy Father informed of the death of Bishop Francis Gleeson sends, to those who know him, an assurance of prayers for the repose of his soul. Giving thanks to God for Bishop Gleeson's many years of faithful proclamation of the Gospel, the Holy Father imparts an Apostolic Blessing to the Diocese of Fairbanks and to all who mourn his death.

After reading the telegram, Bishop Whelan recounted some of the incidents in life that he had shared with Bishop Gleeson. Among other stories he told of the first Pontifical High Mass the Bishop said in Juneau. Neither Gleeson nor Whelan had any experience in this liturgy so they spent some time studying the rubrics. After the Mass they walked to the hospital for lunch. Father Whelan remarked that being new to the hospital finding the way to the cafeteria must be, for the bishop, a little like the recent Mass. Gleeson's answer: *Oooh noo. This time we know where we're going.*

After the Requiem Mass the long cortege rolled quietly through the streets of Fairbanks passing Immaculate Conception Church, The Sisters of Providence deserted hospital building, Monroe High School, and Immaculate Conception Elementary School. On Illinois Street in front of the schools, the students and faculty stood in silent respect.

The Bishop lies facing Fairbanks at the top of a hill in Birch Hill cemetery.

FRONTIERSMAN FOR GOD

Introibo ad altare Dei, I go unto the altar of God; to God who gives joy to my youth. So Father Francis Doyle Gleeson spoke the first time he approached the altar as a priest. Archbishop Hurley recalled this in his remarks at the funeral Mass. *"To God who gives joy to my youth," the joy that was a constant mark of this man noted for his ready wit, the youth displayed by this man who traveled by dogsled, boat and plane the frontier land of Alaska for twenty years.*

For twenty years he defied poverty, arranged for the building of churches and schools, listened to people's troubles and tried to bring comfort to them, body and soul. He did his best to bring understanding and compassion as well as the materials needed to further God's Church and to raise the spirits of the poor, the bewildered, and the desperate.

As Vicar Apostolic and as Bishop of the Diocese of Fairbanks, Bishop Gleeson welcomed any priest who came to him for help. After the Second World War, demobilized chaplains, in particular, found it difficult to adjust. Later, the unsettling events of the "Flower Child" and Vietnam era eroded priestly confidence. To those who came he offered counsel, support, belief and trust. Several of them stayed and worked in

Alaska for a number of years. After that a few left the priesthood for marriage or entered professions which gradually diminished their priestly functions. He looked profoundly sad as he said, *They lost their idealism somewhere.*

One of the priests working at Copper Valley who sought a dispensation asked to have Bishop Gleeson preside at his wedding ceremony in the chancery chapel. Then on the wedding day he was so flustered that he neglected to order flowers for the altar. The bishop noticed and had flowers and decorations arranged so that the bridal couple found everything tastefully prepared for them. Later, the Catholic School Board offered the young man a position as principal of Monroe High School despite the policy of refusal adopted by many bishops. He credits Bishop Gleeson with making the position available to him.

Bishop Gleeson's compassion also saved the reputation of a teacher who gave birth during the school year. No one knew she was married and the consequent general gasp of indignation would have dismissed her from teaching immediately. The bishop refused to pre-judge her. Again, when two young men, superior students in the senior class, would have been expelled for a tasteless, anti-authoritarian prank during the last weeks of the school year, Bishop Gleeson's intervention saved their excellent scholastic and community standing. Sister George Edmond, a Sister of St. Ann, named his compassion as a quality people felt at once. It supported his understanding, serenity, and quiet authority. People felt safe, sheltered, and self-confident in his presence.

It was fitting that he be God's advocate in this frontier land. He brought to it a determination to refurbish the church buildings, and a sure knowledge that his Native people must come to know those who were moving into their land. They must know and understand the language, the customs, the size and difference of the world and the people outside of their sphere. He saw as well that the people of that outside world must accept the Natives as peers and become involved in educating them as leaders.

Years before the Second Vatican Council Gleeson opened consultor meetings to all the Jesuit missionaries of Alaska interested in being present. He pioneered lay teachers in the Catholic schools, the Lay Volunteer in Alaska mission work, and he spoke for a Permanent Diaconate where needed in the United States. He was a forerunner in Alaska in mixed ethnic education and socio economic support for the laity. He championed statehood for the Territory, and to the last year of his episcopacy moved the diocese into the policies formulated by the Second Vatican Council.

Did he have a weakness? Of course. He believed too much in the self-direction of the new priests working in the diocese, and consequently, sometimes gave too little direction and leadership. He was too confident that the leadership he appointed would lead well and competently. He believed strongly in the education of the Native people; yet, he did not provide for an educational plan to direct the inexperienced teachers. At times, he clung too tightly and perhaps too long to managerial authority. Although he could laugh at himself, he was insensitive at times to those who could not laugh at themselves. He did not make himself very visible to the laity, but was easily approached when someone wished to see him.

His constant monetary need may have moved him to listen more to those who could finance their ideas than to those with ideas and no money. Perhaps he did appreciate the ideas presented but did not have the financial means to allow the project. Then, too, perhaps the idea was too far ahead of the time and had to wait for Church approval. Oh, yes, he was thoroughly human. In short, he was a mover and a shaker, but not necessarily one who initiated projects or wrote a scenario for their fulfillment.

BIBLIOGRAPHY

Alaska Milepost. Alaska Northwest Publishing Company, 1983. Annual.

Farquhar, Frank S. Yakima Yesterdays, Yakima Herald Republic, publisher, 1968.

History of Carroll County, Missouri. St. Louis, MO, Historical Company, 1881.

Kleinfeld, Judith. Eskimo School on the Andreafsky, Praeger Publishers, NY, 1979.

Llorente, Segundo, S.J. Jesuits in Alaska, Printed by Key Litho, Portland, Oregon, 1969.

McCullough, Nicole. Red Salmon, Red Scare, The Story of Father Jules Convert and the Bristol Bay Controversy of 1951. University of Alaska, 1996. Ms.

Naske, Claus-M. and Ludwig J. Rowinski. Alaska A Pictorial History, The Donning Company, 1983.

344

Renner, Louis L., S.J. Catholic Ecclesiastical Jurisdiction in Alaska. Ms.

A CHRONICLE OF THE CATHOLIC CHURCH IN THE SEWARD PENINSULA AREA OF ALASKA. MS.

"Father Francis M. Monroe, S.J.," Alaska Magazine, April 1979.

Schoenberg, Wilfred P., S.J. Paths to the Northwest, Loyola University Press, 1982.

House Publications

The Alaskan Shepherd.

The Oregon Jesuit, "Northern Lights on Alaskan News".

Yakima: A Centennial Perspective, 1895-1985.

Interviews and archives.

ABOUT THE AUTHOR

Carol Louise Hiller, O.P. after several years of teaching in elementary schools, altered her educational emphasis to high school librarian. As a librarian she lived in Fairbanks, Alaska and worked at Monroe High School. During her last two years at Monroe, Bishop Whelan requested Bishop Gleeson to speak about his life and work, especially as Shepherd of the Church in Alaska, for the sake of an historical record. His recollections along with Church and Jesuit archives and the recollections of his family and many friends and acquaintances form the record.

Presently Sister resides in Salinas, California